SEE YOU SOON

Philippa has written an honest, extremely moving and very helpful account of the tragic struggle they had with their son's drug addiction. Though painful, it is a 'must read' for all parents of teenagers.

Mary Pytches, author and speaker

As a professional Drugs Worker and also a Christian I would highly recommend this book. The aftermath that Philippa and her family experienced was overwhelming. However, what comes out in these pages is the grief for a lost son, hope that Jim's death was for a purpose and the amazing grace of God that has surrounded Philippa and her family.

Vincent Hessey, Substance Misuse Practitioner

With remarkable courage and honesty, Philippa dares to ask the really hard questions about God and his purposes in the face of crippling personal loss. She vulnerably takes the reader to secret parts of her soul and very perceptively explores the experience of bereavement. Through her writing comes the gentle encouragement to find God even in the midst of unexplained and unrelieved suffering. I delight that Jim's story will continue the work of his short life in bringing hope and healing to the hurting, weak and vulnerable. This book will help us all to live in a broken and confusing world.

Tim Barlow, pastor and retired church leader

I met Philippa Skinner and her husband Graeme in 2009 at DrugFam's first Bereaved by Addiction Conference. As bereaved mothers we will forever share the pain of our common sorrow – the loss of a precious son to heroin. Philippa's story touched me deeply – all the more so because she lost one of her twins in early pregnancy, and the birth of her lone twin, Jim, brought a special joy and happiness into Graeme and Philippa's lives. Philippa shares this ordinary family story of 'her boy Jim' with such compelling dignity and honesty. She writes with courage about her grief and takes you with her through the pain of her loss to living with the reality of Jim's death and finally to an acceptance of her grief. As a committed Christian she dares to ask the question many bereaved mums and dads also want to know: 'Where was God in this?' I commend this story to you as possibly it may help you to find answers to questions in your own lives.

Elizabeth Burton-Phillips
Author, Mum Can You Lend Me Twenty Quid?
What drugs did to my family
Founder of DrugFam

This is a book of great beauty. God has spoken to me through Philippa's story and through Jim's life. He was a soldier who fell in the battle; he is part of a greater army now, cheering us on. Thank you Jim and thank you Philippa.

Keith Sinclair, Bishop of Birkenhead

This book is stunning in its raw honesty, clarity of thinking, and willingness to ask the most difficult questions. I'm sure it will be a help to many as they identify with those deep feelings which are so eloquently described.

Dr Diana Forrest, community activist

We all face loss in our lives, expected and unexpected. This is part of the human experience and often so hard to make sense of. Loss affects us in many ways, at many levels and at all stages of our lives. Several writers have commented that grief is the price we pay for love, and perhaps the death of a child is the hardest to bear and can seem almost unendurable.

This book describes in a deeply moving way Philippa's struggle as she attempts to make sense of the death of her beloved son. She articulates so eloquently the need for the world to see Jim as he was, not wishing the circumstances of his death to tarnish the memory of this kind, sensitive, caring, funny young man. This moving narrative will touch the hearts of all who read it.

Yvonne Ross, counsellor and psychotherapist

In describing every aspect of the journey travelled by the mother and father of a young man wounded fatally in his battle with addiction amidst Christian service, Philippa presents a most valuable picture of what life feels like, and how she has coped with loss. In sharing this with a wider circle, she offers a gift of gracious care, especially to others who might, some time, suffer similarly. Others again, even if not to walk the same dark path, can learn and share from the heartfelt writing in this book. I commend it to all, with or without faith, who want to understand better the human condition and wise descriptions of managing the mind and soul through suffering.

Dr Tim Goodacre, Jim's godfather

See You Soon

A mother's story of drugs, grief and hope

PHILIPPA SKINNER

Spoonbill
Publications

First published in Great Britain in 2012

Published and distributed by Presence Books,
in partnership with Spoonbill Publications:
www.seeyousoon.me.uk

The author and publisher have made every effort to ensure that the external
website and email addresses included in this book are correct and up to date
at the time of going to press. The author and publisher are not responsible
for the content, quality or continuing accessibility of the sites.

Any profit made from the sale of this book will be donated
to St Stephen's Society in Hong Kong and DrugFam in the UK.
For more information about these charities go to:
www.ststephenssociety.com, www.drugfam.co.uk.

Extra information about this book and the issues it raises may be found at
www.seeyousoon.me.uk.

Song 'May the words of my mouth', Tim Hughes and Rob Hill.
Copyright © 2000, Thankyou Music/Adm. by worshiptogether.com.
Songs excl. UK and Europe adm. by kingswaysongs, a division of
David C. Cook tym@kingsway.co.uk. Used by permission.

Cover photos

Front cover: Jim Skinner, Hong Kong lights and the memorial garden at
St Stephen's Society community houses, Shing Mun Springs, Shatin,
Hong Kong.
Back cover: Rainbow over Hong Kong tower blocks.
Images: Graeme Skinner

British Library Cataloguing-in-Publication Data
A catalogue record for this book is available from the British Library

ISBN 978-1-907228-29-2

Typeset by Caroline Waldron, Wirral, Cheshire
Printed in England by Imprint Digital, Exeter, Devon.

Printed on recycled paper.

Contents

Dedicated to all my family,
who have gone through this with me.
I love you.

Foreword

This is the foreword I had hoped never to write. Remembering dear Jim and the terrible way his life ended is something I had no wish to think of or remember. Yet it is a story that must be told. The Bible would never have been written if we had not sinned, but God had planned salvation from the beginning of time and caused His heart to be written down, so that by believing that Jesus is the Christ we may have life.

I feel privileged that Jim's parents have invited me to share this introduction, and privileged to have known Jim and to have walked a while with him and his family.

When I first knew Jesus my faith was simple but also simplistic. The problem was – I had the wrong version of the Bible! Mine read, 'When anyone is in Christ, he is a new man' (2 Corinthians 5.17). Therefore when, wonderfully, the first drug addict I prayed for accepted Jesus, sang with awe and then prayed in tongues for half an hour I thought the job was done. He was a new man, could go to work the next day and glorify Christ. He would not need or want drugs again. He had Jesus.

Many believers in Christ think similarly, and so find it hard to understand the 'new man' when he stumbles. Some of us think that more Bible, more prayer, more counselling or more hard work would prevent failure, but we have misunderstood the problem. 'When anyone is in Christ he is a new *creation*' is a better understanding of the text. This 'new creation' may be quite old in years (and will certainly have old habits and old clothes) but he really needs a safe place to grow up at his own pace; to grow up emotionally, spiritually, to put off the old self and then to grow in hope for the future.

At St Stephen's Society we have seen hundreds of men and women from their teens to their seventies who have lived with us and changed dramatically. My husband John was a heroin addict who, once he met Jesus, never took drugs again or wanted them. He fell in love with Christ and worshipped his way to wholeness. However, it took many more years for him to grow into maturity and deal with who he was, what God thought about him and what he believed about himself.

Yes, we have seen hundreds delivered physically from drugs by the power of the Holy Spirit, but now know that is the easy part. The next is longer and different for every person. One person may deal quickly with their past while others need time, but we love them just the same, and if they leave us before the knots are sorted out, we worry. Some will die. The knots have become a noose. Then we cry, we howl, we grieve and go through many of the same emotions and experiences which Philippa so graphically describes in this book.

Years ago, a friend helped me to understand the problem. I felt I couldn't share the amazing stories of some of the addicts from the Walled City because they had fallen later. 'Why not?' he asked. 'What Jesus did for them is just as wonderful – isn't it?' And so I learned that in the gospel stories we rarely know how those that Jesus healed went on afterwards. The gospels just record what Jesus did and how the sick, demonized and outcast responded.

Jim always responded to Jesus in his spirit. He loved Him and was incredibly brave in allowing himself to be forgiven and to hope again. In this heartbreaking story you will meet a young man whom everyone thought to be their own special friend and who brought joy and fun to many.

This book is written to bring healing and resolution to those who, like Philippa and Graeme, may ask 'Why?' It is an account written with courage and honesty, reflecting the awful pain of loss and untimely death. Yet with conviction that Jim's life was not in vain and that his story would bring healing to many, they have shared their journey of healing.

I have dealt with my own guilt as have Jim's parents. We would all like to blame someone, but the fact is that the enemy felled Jim in battle. A glorious young warrior in training became a prime target. But I believe that his life (and death) will bring life to many. Through the cross there is redemption. The enemy will not have victory (1 Corinthians 15.26). The last enemy to be destroyed is death. Through this story I know there will be many who will sing 'Thank God for Jesus and for Jim' (1 Corinthians 15.54). Death has been swallowed up in victory.

Jackie Pullinger
St Stephen's Society, Hong Kong

Introduction

What follows is a true story but not an autobiography. It is the story of one part of our family life which has caused me to dig deep into my resources to discover if survival was an option. That sounds dramatic, I know, but after all survival comes in many forms beyond the merely physical.

Bereavement is part of all of our lives in any number of ways, from the obvious one of separation from loved ones by death, to divorce, retirement and loss of health, to name but a few, and many of the feelings of bereavement are universal. While what follows concentrates on physical bereavement, it may be that some of the emotions expressed will be familiar to those who have experienced loss in different ways.

When our son, Jim, died from a heroin overdose at the age of 21, Graeme and I were thrust into a new and deeply confusing world in which we could find few signposts to guide us on our way. The world we thought we knew became altogether darker and more dangerous.

Perhaps I can liken the experience as suddenly moving from sunshine to thick, swirling fog, or discovering that the ground you thought you could trust has suddenly given way beneath your feet to reveal a huge, yawning chasm. Anyone who has experienced sudden, traumatic loss of whatever kind may have an inkling of what I mean, though each person will find their own way to describe it.

I tried to find help to guide me through this new, terrifyingly unfamiliar terrain in a number of different ways. One of the first of these was by buying and reading as many books on bereavement as I thought I could cope with. Some of these were extremely helpful and I remain ever grateful to the authors. I discovered through the stories of other people that many had walked this way, and had survived. This was good news, though in the early days it was hard to believe that it would also be true for me or us. For now, those books remained something to hang on to, to turn to for encouragement, and a way to understand that what we were experiencing was not unique. Although it felt as if the landscape of our world was changed for ever and we were lost, others had walked similar ways and had left signposts on how to live.

As I negotiated my way through those dreadfully dark days, helped by many wise words, there remained some unanswered questions. How were we to reconcile the hopes, dreams and prayers made by us for our family over three decades for their protection and future lives, with the devastating and, as we saw it, degrading death of our son in a downbeat apartment in Hong Kong from an overdose of heroin? Where was God in all this? Was he there at all, or had those prayers been like chaff, wasted and carried away by the wind? If we were unable to reconcile our doubts, then how could we, with integrity, carry on in our present lives, with Graeme leading a local church with the responsibility for preaching and teaching a message of good news and hope?

Other questions sprang from this. If God was there and did care and had heard our prayers, despite the terrible outcome, what should we learn from this dreadful event? My previous life experiences had already shaped me into a person who believed that God can and does use us in our weakness, but now I felt a new depth of brokenness, and saw my usually resilient husband emotionally battered and bruised in such a deep way that he was almost like a different person for some time. Was it possible that there was still work to do for a couple who felt such abject failures in their family life, the part of their life they cared most about?

There was another question too, always lurking in the recesses of my hurting mind and spirit. Did anyone really care that my son had died? Because he had died of a heroin overdose, did people secretly feel that it was his fault and he wasn't worth much sympathy? No book that I found then seemed to address the painful area of loss by addiction and I could find no help at all in dealing with this question. As time has gone on, I have discovered by personal experience, and subsequently in discussion with others, that such bereavement carries its own particular difficulties that are hard to live with, especially in the area of shame and stigma.

In his last letter to us, written a few weeks before he died, Jim concluded, 'See you soon (relatively)'. These few words, written in the expectation that we would soon go to visit him in Hong Kong where he was then living, became very poignant as we grappled with despair and tried to find hope for a meaningful future. What does it mean to grieve as Christian people, in the light of St Paul's words that we were not to grieve as those who had no hope? How do we live, caught between the despair of loss and the hope one day of being reunited with our loved ones? Though my faith might teach that I would see Jim again one day, I couldn't do what I wanted, which was to see him now and to hug him. The promise of 'one day' brought scant comfort, I found, just as I couldn't make myself feel warmer in the bone-chill of dead winter simply by knowing that one day spring will come.

It is in an attempt to look at these questions and to discover some necessarily partial and personal answers that I offer this reflection on Jim, grief, drugs and hope. Maybe it will reach out to those who have been bereaved and will help them in the same way I was helped by books. Maybe it will give some insight to others who have not experienced traumatic loss but want to help a friend or family member struggling with bereavement. I pray that it will keep company with those who have lost, or fear losing, loved ones to addictions of various kinds. Above all, I hope that when other parents find themselves flung into that dark and devastating world of child loss, and wonder if they can survive, it may provide them with a few signposts in the fog to help them keep going, in the same way as I was given signposts by others.

To look at these issues, it has been necessary to tell some of Jim's and our family story, not because it is unique for of course all our stories are unique, or because I think it is more deserving than anyone else's story, but merely because it is the environment from which the questioning grew. I often wonder what Jim, a private and self-effacing young man, would make of it, but I like to think he would forgive me for sharing aspects of our story that were never meant to be shared, and, as was his habit, come up quietly behind me, lay his hand on my shoulder and say gently in his quiet but deep Manchester accent, 'I lov' you, mom'.

CHAPTER 1

Ordinary Lives

How blessed we are, when we are secure and life is routine.

'Did anything happen today?'

'No, not really, just the normal.'

Maybe we settle down at the end of such a day, grab a bite to eat and a glass of something, reach for the TV controls, and look for a dose of vicarious excitement through soaps or dramas of one kind or another, to switch off from the often mundane demands of our working day. I suppose we don't often stop to think what a blessing it is to live a day and end it safely, knowing that all our loved ones are also safe. It is only when that secure and safe life is suddenly turned upside down and real-life drama and tragedy crash into your world, that you appreciate the blessing of ordinary days. At least, that was how it felt to me when Jim died, out of the blue, of a heroin overdose. Thrown into a new and dark world, I would have given anything to have my routine life back but, in some ways, those days have gone for ever, and maybe part of the learning, for me, has been to learn gratitude for ordinary days, and to live more fully in them. I am still learning what this means – and always will be.

The following story is one of ordinary lives . . . a regular family, which would have ticked most of the boxes if we were being measured for unremarkability. I write it now simply to tell of my love for Jim and to encourage other ordinary families out there, where events have taken an unexpected turn, where you may be tempted to wonder what went wrong and whether you can still trust God to be God.

Beginnings

Most people will agree that being a parent is one of the hardest jobs around, if not the hardest. Becoming a parent can be hard enough, but being a parent – that is something else. Once you are a parent, there is no eight-hour working day, no sick leave, no pension plan, no rights at all really; just lots of hard work, physical and emotional. Oh . . . and the other thing about the job . . . there is no training for it. When you think about it, it's a wonder so many of us willingly choose this demanding path, and yet, despite all sorts of social, environmental, financial and political changes going on around us which might make us think at least twice about such a huge decision, we often do.

For me, family life felt very important; and for some, no doubt deep psychological reason, I was keen to have a relatively large family. I'm inclined to think part of the reason was because as a child I spent too long reading Enid Blyton and E. Nesbit books where all the kids seemed to have endless fun and adventures. I rather fancied a large, cheerful brood who played together and created their own adventures. I hope there were some more profound reasons too, but who really knows? The end result was that within eight years of marriage we had four children: girl, boy, boy, girl – a kind of boy sandwich. Hannah and Chloe were the bread, so to speak, and Tom and Jim the filling!

My rather romantic ideas of the childhood my children would enjoy were not entirely misplaced. While few of their adventures would have lived up to the joy of finding a psammead and growing wings or becoming invisible for the day, the early years included a lot of fun – along with all the common daily trials, too numerous to mention. I, though never much of an 'earth mother' sort, enjoyed my role mostly and chose to be a stay-at-home mum in the early years. In truth, back in the 1980s there wasn't much choice anyway, especially if there was no chance of help from an extended family and you were regularly on the move, as we were with five different homes in ten years. Anyway, it suited me in many ways. I liked being around the children and I held the lofty opinion that I didn't want to pay anyone to do something I reckoned I could do better myself!

Introducing Jim

Jim was our third child, four years younger than Hannah and two years younger than Tom, almost precisely. Carrying Jim wasn't an easy time for me. In the early weeks of the pregnancy, I had a miscarriage and was devastated by the experience. I felt very angry with myself, as if somehow it was my fault. I felt so sad and disappointed even though I knew I was blessed in having two lovely children already. That little baby, who I had begun to care about and build a proto-relationship with, was lost, and it really hurt. Strangely, however, as the days passed I realised I still felt pregnant. For a while we assumed it was just the effect of pregnancy hormones still circulating in my body but after a few weeks I discovered that in actual fact I was still pregnant. I had been carrying twins and one of the babies had been lost while the other – who would become Jim – remained. I felt a mixture of emotions now – joy and relief tempered with anxiety for the remaining baby. I could not help fearing that the miscarriage and the trauma around that event would have in some way harmed him or her. A friend, older than us and wiser in many ways, with the wonderful name of Mrs Angel, came and prayed for us at this time and she gave us these words of prophecy, which I treasured immediately and never let go. 'The baby will be a soldier and servant of the Lord and the joy of his salvation will be his strength and his song.' I hung on to these words through all the months and years ahead and they remained special and a great encouragement, though I could not begin to understand their full significance until another 21 years had passed. The rest of the pregnancy was mostly uneventful, though part of me always feared that the baby would have been damaged by the early brush with death when its brother or sister was lost.

Jim finally arrived ten days late, on 7th January 1986, having narrowly missed being a Christmas baby. He made his way uneventfully into the world and it was a joyful day when we got to meet him for the first time and bring him home to his sister and brother. He was a big and bouncing baby as it happened, and I needn't have wasted so much time worrying over the previous nine months. Despite the vast amount of stress hormones I had probably passed on to young Jim while he was still in the womb, he was a peaceful little fellow, who adopted a laid-back attitude to life from an early age, observing with great interest all the antics of his older siblings and generally making sure he got his full quota of attention by quickly developing some very winning ways.

Two years later, also in January, Chloe was born and our family was complete.

In those early years they were a cheerful little band, brought up quite traditionally. In the 1980s and early 1990s there was little technology available: no computers, no DVDs, no mobile phones and not even any day-time children's TV to talk of. Instead it was a time of picture books, jigsaws, dressing up and endless home-made games and plays. It seems very simple now, looking back just a few years.

While I was busy having babies, Graeme was training for ministry in the Church of England and by 1990 he was the vicar of a large and demanding parish in the south of Manchester. There were all sorts of unexpected challenges for which, to be honest, neither of us had the experience. Still, I suppose being thrown in the deep end is one way of learning. We gained a few bumps and bruises along the way but we survived and in time we came to love that place and the people there, who showed us remarkable grace and patience as we all grew together. It was to be our home for sixteen years, a time of great stability for us after the years of moving around. We were blessed in having a pleasant home provided as part of the job, and it gave the family a great place in which to grow up. I was so grateful for our home, it became a very special place to us, and Sale and the people of the parish became part of our lives and our hearts over those busy years. Many important relationships were formed then and endure now.

Hard times

It is tempting to pop on the rose-coloured specs when remembering the past. There were many good times and it is great to recall these, but the reality is often to be found somewhere in-between, because of course there were also hard things to cope with. There were grim patches where I battled with depression, guilt and anxiety linked mostly, I believe, to watching my mother change so much with an unusual form of dementia, which developed over several years until she was unable to respond to us or even, as far as we knew, recognise us. Irrationally, I felt such terrible guilt about her situation, especially when she needed to be moved into a nursing home near us. It was truly heartbreaking to witness her decline and deep unhappiness. She was never able to play with or enjoy her lovely grandchildren, which always seemed so sad to me. She would have loved them. She finally died aged 64, when Chloe, the youngest, was two years old and Hannah was eight. I really struggled for some three years after she died, as I grieved for all the lost years of her life and the terrible pain she had endured, as well as grieving for her actual loss.

Looking after four young children and doing my best to support Graeme who was coming to terms with life in a very busy parish, while grieving for my mother and being in a new community, left its mark on me. Spiritually and emotionally, there is no doubt that Graeme and I were both running on empty and were in urgent need of refreshment. Eventually in the summer of 1993 we found our way to New Wine, in those days merely a summer holiday and conference week arranged by St Andrew's Church, Chorleywood, where I had grown up.[1]

I was utterly convinced I wouldn't like it; 'Camping – with 6,000 people on a dodgy camp site? Not my kind of thing at all,' I thought. Still, I think God must have known better than me because finally, having been encouraged many times by some dear friends to go, and wriggling out of it by saying we had no camping equipment, we put down a kind of 'Gideon's fleece' ultimatum. We decided that if we put an advert in the church newsletter asking to borrow a tent and enough associated paraphernalia for six of us, that we would go if we had an offer. I thought it highly unlikely that anyone would be willing to trust so much to us, but in fact the offer, rather to my dismay, had been made by lunchtime of the same day the advert appeared! So that was that. Off we went a few weeks later, down the M6, looking remarkably like the Larkin family from *Darling Buds of May*, in our overloaded Peugeot 505, plus borrowed trailer. Fortunately the children were still young enough to think this was just another adventure, rather than be horribly embarrassed by us!

We benefited hugely from the spiritual encouragement we found there, and I discovered that it was well worth a week of relative discomfort to enjoy all that the conference had to offer through excellent teaching and passionate worship. We needed this after some lean years. Our warm relationship with New Wine was sealed by the evident enjoyment of the children, who lapped it all up and were keen to return year after year. To see them being fed so well spiritually and growing in their own faith, as well as having a great time running around in comparative freedom, was wonderful for us. We owe a great deal to the New Wine movement which has developed hugely since those early years and has continued to be a major part of our support as the years have passed.

Back at home, prayers were said every day, one to one with our children and together as a couple. Often when I prayed for the family, I had two pictures: one was of holding the children out to God on an open hand, in the hope that I would be willing to trust him with them, and be ready to let them go when the time came; the other was of four lights in the darkness as I prayed that one day they would live for Jesus wherever they went, and that their lives would be lights in a hurting world.

Jim grows up

One of the joys of family life, I think, is seeing how we all find our place and fill different roles in the unit without even trying; it just happens. Each child had a very different personality and they each added to our family life in their own unique way.

In the family videos Jim was the dancing, jigging one and would pull the most ridiculous faces whenever the camera appeared. He had his own unique way of coining new words and phrases that would sometimes leave us in stitches. He was that strange and hard to resist mixture of gentle and mischievous. He was, though he wouldn't thank me for writing it, cute, and he quickly became a favourite of the girls in his primary school. He was quick to learn to play to his strengths and had a great capacity for being naughty and then getting off lightly by blinking at you, wide-eyed and apparently innocently, through the glasses he had worn since the age of three. He was a tree-climbing, football-playing, bike-riding boy, just fun to be with in all sorts of ways. Yes, a monkey, who could wrap you round his little finger – but a very lovable monkey, at least to his mum.

I often think of those years when the children were older

than babies but had not yet hit puberty as the golden years, but things can't stay the same for ever and I know I am fortunate and am grateful that I have so many good memories. The years roll on of course, and through happy times, sad times, busy times, holiday times, stretching and growing times, we all developed as a family from pre-school days and young parenthood to those new experiences of living with and trying to understand teenagers – and, equally hard, living with and trying to understand your parents. Both roles require a high degree of grace and tolerance it seems to me. If I failed to understand where my teenage children were coming from, too often, I have no doubt I must have seemed just as mysterious and hard to fathom to them. If only real life could be more like the Blyton and Nesbit books I had loved as a child, where the sun always shines and endings are only happy.

Still, Graeme and I hoped that in the real world, through faith, love and example, we had built a strong enough foundation for each child so that they would be able to stand up to the inevitable pressures the teenage years would bring. I really did believe in the power of love, and though family life and relationships became considerably more turbulent and demanding, I continued to trust that each child would find their way and ultimately pass safely through the tunnel that can be adolescence. Mistakes are inevitable along the way – wrong decisions, angry words said in haste you later regret; but I suppose we just tried, like so many other parents in so many other situations, to do our best, knowing that often we failed ourselves and our children. Then it was a matter of saying sorry and starting again, as well as needing to forgive ourselves for not being as perfect as we would have liked to have been. So much of this life seems to be about trying, falling over, getting up and trying again, and so much seems to be about learning to forgive ourselves and others when things don't go as we want.

CHAPTER 2

Teenage Years

Hard questions

I wonder how many times I have asked the question 'Why?' over the past three years. Why did Jim start smoking cannabis, a decision that I believe ultimately led to his early death four years later? Maybe a reasonable answer is 'Why not?' After all, so many young people get hold of drugs, and Jim was just an ordinary lad, part of an ordinary family. I would love to be able to sit with him and ask him the question now, to try and understand and hear the reasons in his own words – if indeed he himself really knew what they were. The truth is, cannabis is out there, along with many other potentially harmful substances, so easily available – a truth I have become increasingly aware of. Once I was fairly naïve, but now I smell it frequently, wherever I might be . . . in the street, in a park, even coming from a passing car's window. It's sold outside the school gate and it's sold within schools as well. It doesn't matter which school either, fee-paying or the local high school. You can't pay money to protect your child or move to a 'better area' to try and escape. It is just there. This is part of our culture.

A vast number of our young people experiment at some time with the drug, and many use it or other drugs recreationally. It is part of the social scene – something that people do. The British Crime Survey 2008–9 tells us that nearly one in five young people aged between 16 and 24 took the drug in the year prior to the survey, and of these over one in three took it more than once a month.[1] That's a lot of young people.

Statistics mean very little when you are considering individual lives, of course, and they don't provide any answers, except to tell us there is nothing unusual in getting hold of cannabis. As parents of a growing family we were aware of the risks of drugs, were careful to read the leaflets about them, learnt their street names and the signs and symptoms to look for; but when it came down to it, none of this made any difference. We did our best to warn our children of the dangers and we also knew that the best way to protect your child was to keep a good relationship with them and to be available to them, talking about the things they want to talk about, accepting that that meant a lot of listening to their views, and knowing that as far as they were concerned you didn't know or understand very much as a mere adult.

In the years since Jim has died we have naturally thought a great deal about the subject of why people take drugs, and in particular, why Jim took drugs. I'm not an expert and it is not appropriate or possible for me to examine the question of drug use in general in any depth here, but we have found Jackie Pullinger's explanation, given in a series of talks at a conference we attended, as helpful a way as any to think about the problem.[2] Jackie explained, using an analogy from geology, that rather like the earth's crust we all have fault-lines, which can be thought of as weak areas or cracks which we may be unaware of from day to day. As we encounter difficulties in our lives of any kind – bereavement, relationship stress, unemployment, loneliness or even the stress of changing from a child to an adult – these fault-lines may become more obvious. It becomes harder for us to cope. We may then turn to any one of a number of coping mechanisms, some of which could be harmless, like losing ourselves in a good book, or some of which may have the potential to cause us damage such as over- or under-eating, compulsive exercising or turning to drugs or alcohol. No doubt this is too simple to be the explanation, and there will be many possible answers to the same question, all with a measure of truth; but I find it one helpful way to think about it, nevertheless. In my opinion, it enables others like me who haven't succumbed to drug or alcohol abuse to recognise our own coping mechanisms and to be honest about how we too have areas of weakness. It is one way of looking at the question 'Why?' which lowers the barriers between those who develop drug and alcohol problems and those who don't.

To return to the question of why Jim, in particular, started with drugs, I think the honest answer is – he just did. On that day he must have felt curious enough, anxious to fit in with his group enough, maybe insecure enough to just give it a go. The drug was there, being offered . . . what harm could it do? Maybe it felt exciting to him to kick over the traces a little and do something a bit reckless. I don't think there was any dark, inner reason; it just happened. What I have since learnt, though, is that no one knows who will be particularly vulnerable to the effects of drug use. I know there are many who argue that cannabis is not addictive, and maybe physiologically it isn't, but psychologically it is surely a different matter.[3] I know of many people now whose lives have been severely impacted by a cannabis habit. It is far from a harmless substance, especially in the more modern form of skunk, which is two or three times stronger than the cannabis that was commonly smoked in previous decades. It has potentially major implications for those who experiment with it. I'm not an expert and don't try to be – I just know what I know anecdotally; and above all, I know what it led to eventually for Jim.

Learning together

As it happened, Jim had a lot of opinions on a lot of subjects and he wasn't shy about sharing them. Sometimes he would be silent or monosyllabic like many an adolescent, but other times he would let rip, giving us the benefit of exactly what he thought about capitalism and Marxism, the education system, Christianity, President Bush, the future, and anything else that was on his mind. He enjoyed walking our dog, Bessie, with us at the weekends, and these were often the times, when it was just the three of us, that he would open up and really get talking on a great variety of subjects. It was quite hard work keeping up with it all sometimes, but we were pleased he felt able to chat like this, so we didn't stop him. What fired him up above all else was injustice and hypocrisy, as he understood it then. Not all his opinions at age sixteen or so were very wise, but at least they were sincere!

Nor were all his decisions very wise. I remember one day discovering a tube of ointment for haemorrhoid relief on the bathroom shelf. Since I didn't recognise it, I was intrigued to say the least. It seemed an unlikely bathroom accessory in a house of teenagers. I suggested to Graeme he might like to do some undercover work and find out what was going on, as I had already worked out that Jim was the probable owner, and I guessed he would prefer to speak to his father rather than his mother on such a delicate topic!

It turned out that Jim had paid a visit to the local tattoo parlour that day and had asked to be decorated with a large, rather bold image of Che Guevara on his upper arm. The piles ointment was recommended by the tattooist in case the wound subsequently got infected or itchy. Our response to the news of his tattoo may perhaps be imagined, but the deed was done now so there wasn't a great deal we could do or say. When asked 'Why Che?', Jim responded in typical Jim fashion, that Che was a man of conviction, and even if you didn't agree with everything he did, you at least had to admire him for sticking to his principles. So there we were, stuck with Che Guevara as part of our family. The next day, brimming with indignation that the tattoo parlour had seen fit to perform such an act on the under-age arm of our quite small and young-looking sixteen-year-old son, I burst into the shop demanding an explanation. I like to think the brawny shaven-headed man in charge there was taken aback by this vision of motherly outrage. Well, perhaps he was, but not much could be done now, except for making a few idle threats to report the business. Jim meanwhile was in skin-level fellowship with Che for the next few years. A couple of years later he tried to balance things up by getting another tattoo, this time of a cross, on his ankle. I think he realised by then that actually Jesus was a better role model for him.

At the time that Jim got his first tattoo we had four ado-lescents in the house – and only one bathroom. It was a truly testing time of life, but also very stimulating – all those young people developing into who they were made to be, each one with unique gifts and character. For me, however, they were the hardest years of parenting, the ones that brought me most challenges as I struggled to keep up with all the changes in our family life.

These days I sit in a well-ordered house that is often very quiet. When I go into the bathroom or the living-room I know they will be how I left them. The washing basket is slow to fill up, and shop-ping trips look very grown up as I fill the trolley with the things I like, rather than mass purchases to keep hungry young people satisfied. Muddy sports clothes left in the wrong place and school bags dumped in the hallway where they were dropped no longer need to be negotiated. Bedrooms that look like the aftermath of a passing tornado are just fond memories. There are always gains and losses in every situation, and it is certainly very dif-ferent these days. There was a kind of lively chaos then, created by six people, four of them, at least, with busy social lives, who usually managed to come together for an evening meal.

I kept my sanity – or maybe tested it even more – by studying and becoming a teacher over these years. It was good to have something else to put my mind to, rather than being swallowed up by the many demands of home. It wasn't easy studying with so much going on around me, but I remember, with great fondness, Jim's pride in me and for me when I finally qualified.

Jim had some struggles. He didn't enjoy school too much despite being a bright lad. At the age of fifteen or sixteen he expressed a desire to leave and get an apprenticeship or go to the local college of further education and explore courses that might lead him to a career in the Army. We went with him when he checked the options out, but when he looked into it, it became clear to him that he wasn't very suited to such things. For now, it felt better to stick with school and study for A-levels, which he did with only a little reluctance. Over the final two years of schooling we witnessed a slow blossoming of our boy, as he found to his surprise that he actually enjoyed his studies. Before I knew it I needed to call on rather rusty memories to engage with him on matters historical and literary. He was very taken with the classics and we had many happy times discussing his course books. I admit in my case it was rather a bluff as it was a long time since I had read the texts, but he seemed happy to share his new-found knowledge, and I was happy to spend time with him in this way, or by watching films and documentaries on areas of interest to him. Once we persuaded him to come with us to visit the Bronte Parsonage in Haworth and the supposed site of the farm house, 'Wuthering Heights', to help him to engage with his A-level book. I remember he commented how long it was since he had been with us for a day out, how much he had enjoyed it and how he intended to do it more often! Graeme found that his chief area of communication was via mutual enjoyment of sport, and in particular, rugby. He and the boys spent many cold and muddy Fridays and Saturdays eating meat pies and supporting our local team, Sale Sharks.

In all the ups and downs of muddling through with a household of adolescents, there were some grand times. Very importantly, they were times of learning for us as much as the growing children, and that learning took many forms. At this point Graeme was discovering the cell church movement and trying to pass on and put into practice some of the concepts in our own church. I was working as an ESOL (English to speakers of other languages) teacher and enjoying the challenge of being involved with many people from troubled parts of the world who were trying to adapt to a new life in England, and at the same time we were learning how to parent a house of rumbustious teenagers. Never a dull moment!

As conscientious parents we had read appropriate books and attended seminars at New Wine and through Care for the Family to help us in our task of bringing up the family. While it never seems so simple in real life, we did learn some important principles which helped along the way. The importance of setting boundaries, keeping communication lines open, willingness to trust your teenager as far as possible, and not working against each other as parents, are some of the most valuable ones. As we have looked back, we often remind ourselves that as parents we did our best, which is all any of us can be asked to do. Our best is flawed in many ways but it is still all we can do, as we offer to God who we are and ask him to be with us in all those daily tasks and decisions that require so much wisdom.

Uncomfortable truths

It has often been remarked that it is difficult to tell the difference between normal teenage behaviour and behaviour related to drug use. This was true in our case. Even after lots of soul searching and self-questioning, we are still unable to know how we could have told that Jim was messing around with cannabis until we discovered it hidden in his room. Jim was a regular guy, attending school, holding down newspaper rounds and other small jobs, building relationships, and often very good fun to be with. Then there was the other side – the uncertain, gauche teenager, somewhat small for his age, rather insecure in himself, longing to be more than he was . . . bigger, bolder and braver. He was brave of course – though we only realised how brave as a few more years passed. We had the anxieties of many parents of teenagers and often asked ourselves, 'What's wrong with Jim tonight? He seems very quiet/surly/grumpy', and so on. But if you tried to get alongside to ask him if there were any problems, and he wasn't in the mood to chat, you soon knew you were in his bad books. So we would back off, thinking it better to respect him and give him space, hoping he would talk when he was ready to. It isn't easy being the parents of teenagers, is it?

It came as an enormous shock to us, naïve parents that we were, when we accidentally found cannabis hidden in one of Jim's socks, as we sorted out the washing one day, in the spring of 2003, when he was seventeen. Though we had read the books and leaflets, when it came to real life, we felt quite helpless. What were we to do? Who could we ask for advice? None of our friends had ever talked about such things happening in their families and we simply didn't know where to turn. On top of that, there was the matter of confidentiality. We couldn't just talk about it to anyone because we had a relationship with Jim to maintain and he wouldn't thank us if his personal affairs became common knowledge.

Jim's response to us was predictable. 'There isn't a problem . . . I'm in control . . . everyone is doing it . . . you don't understand . . . I don't need help.' He wasn't best pleased with us for finding his stash, nor with us for wanting to talk to him about it. Unhelpfully for us, at about this time the government downgraded the classification of cannabis from a class B drug to a class C, a decision that has now been reversed. Jim used this as further ammunition to shore up his case and show us how out of touch we were. 'Even the government doesn't think it's a problem.' Jim was seventeen, we couldn't force him to do anything he didn't want to do, and we could only engage with him and share honestly why we felt upset and the possible dangers of his behaviour as we understood them. We were anxious not to make Jim feel cornered in such a way that he was put in a defensive mode and would refuse to talk to us any more. Above all, it felt important to try to keep channels of communication open. We came to realise there were some hard times ahead where our learning would go on to a different plane. We did what all Christian parents would do of course: we prayed to God earnestly for Jim, and trusted that despite it all he would be kept safe. We also did our best not to go down paths of despair – cannabis leads to hard drugs leads to death. While we knew little in those days, we did know enough to understand that though we were rightly upset and concerned by our discovery, the statistical probability was that Jim would be OK in the end.

Surprising events

These events happened in early summer and we had a few hard months ahead. The holiday period loomed and Jim made it clear he didn't want to come with us. There was nothing especially unusual in a seventeen-year-old not wanting to go to Cornwall with his parents, but we felt very anxious about leaving him at home on his own. Increasingly, we felt insecure about him and we were worried about what he might get up to in two weeks with no one around. His behaviour wasn't bad or disruptive in any way, but he just seemed subdued and unhappy. Our heartfelt prayers on his behalf continued.

Then out of the blue, to us at least, Jim received a letter from Jackie Pullinger in Hong Kong, inviting him to come and spend a few weeks over the summer with St Stephen's Society, a charity working with the drug addicted and the marginalised. It seemed like the answer to our prayers. Jim's relationship with Jackie had begun in the summer of 2000 when he was fourteen. That year we had all gone to Soul Survivor, in Shepton Mallet. Soul Survivor was born of the New Wine movement and had a particular ministry to young people, and we were going that summer with a few youngsters from our church, including our own family. Jim wasn't too keen on coming with us but we promised him he need not attend any meetings if he didn't want to and could spend the whole time with his skateboard if he preferred, and so we were able to win him over.

God famously moves in mysterious ways, however, and his ways are not ours. While we thought Jim would be happy enough communing with his skateboard, somehow the spirit of the place tempted him to venture out, and before long we were wondering where he was. It happened that he had decided to attend a series of seminars about addiction led by Jackie, and he found himself enthralled. He made himself known to her and in no time he had befriended the team of young men from Hong Kong who accompanied her. He spent most of that week with them, laying down the foundations of some special relationships and eating noodles with his new friends. Over the week he gave his life to Jesus and even gave his testimony of how he had decided to follow Jesus in a meeting of some 4,000 people.

When we returned home, Jim kept the relationship going by writing regularly to his friends in St Stephen's and earning money from his paper round and sending out gifts to the boys. He kept Jackie's book, *Chasing the Dragon*, by his bed and read it many times, along with other popular Christian classics. This went on for three years and explains how, when he was seventeen, he was invited to visit for four weeks.

His initial response was not too promising: 'What's the point of me going? I'm not even a Christian'. I will never forget Jackie's response by email for which I am always grateful, 'Never mind that – just come and do some good'. I was impressed by her openness in inviting this rather lost young man to come and spend time with them even though he wasn't all sorted out. He remained unsure, however, and Graeme and I didn't try to persuade him, one way or the other, as we realised pressure from us might have the opposite outcome to the one we hoped for. We prayed that he would make up his mind to go though, as we really felt it might be significant for him. Eventually, after a few days' thought, he decided to go. We were delighted and also considerably poorer, as last-minute tickets to Hong Kong in the summer season are not cheap. We were sure it was worth digging into our pockets to get him to an environment which would be wholesome and challenging for him – just what our wandering seventeen-year-old needed, we believed, and offered without us looking for it. Surely this was God at work. We prayed hard for him in those four weeks, that he would grow in faith and find a passion which would give him purpose for his life.

One month later and Jim returned, blooming in many ways. His confidence had grown, his faith had grown and – yes – he had found a passion as over those few short weeks he had developed a love for playing the guitar, an interest which brought him much satisfaction in the years ahead. He had been introduced to the work of St Stephen's and made some deep friendships. He had won his way into many people's hearts there and it became clear in an email we received from Jackie before he had even landed at Manchester airport, that there would be a place for him in St Stephen's if he ever chose to go back.

The new school term soon began, and Jim, now in his final year, settled down to his studies, and when he wasn't at school or working in the local Co-op supermarket he was often in his room, practising on the guitar until he began to grow quite accomplished. He was a new person in many ways, and seemed to have grown up so much. It was a real joy to us to see how he was finding out what really mattered to him. Jim had a finely tuned conscience and felt deeply the pain and sadness around him. Over this time he enjoyed visiting some older members of the church whom he cared for particularly. He turned into a most delightful young man. If I had to use a few words to sum him up, as he developed, they would be sensitive, gentle, droll, intelligent and deeply caring. (Well . . . after all I am his mother . . . but I still think they sum him up.) He worked many hours in the shop, where he befriended several regular customers, especially the lonely, the poor and those who came to stock up on their drink supplies. As well as this, he worked in an after-school maths club with young children, another job he enjoyed.

Life, however, is seldom a smooth path upwards, and after a while pressures built up in Jim again – peer pressure, insecurity, self-doubt . . . I'm not sure. Only Jim could answer that, and maybe even he couldn't, as often it is hard for us to understand ourselves and why we feel as we do. Too often there is no obvious answer.

I became suspicious that Jim was using cannabis again a few months after his return from Hong Kong, and one night we found him smoking in his room, his head hanging out of the open window in an attempt to lessen the smell of the drug. Of course he was angry that we had discovered him again, and once again denied there was any problem, telling us that he only felt happy when he was smoking weed – words which sent a shiver down my spine. There was no point in talking to him then, and we went to our bed with heavy hearts. We felt so powerless against the attraction of this supposedly innocuous herb. Whatever he got from smoking, it was seemingly more than he could find without it.

Later that night, however, in the small hours, he came to our bedroom in tears and quite broken. He sobbed that he realised he did have a problem and he didn't want to be like this. He was afraid that he was weak and if he stayed at home and did what most of his other friends were doing, preparing to go to university, he would not be able to break free from the power of the temptation to smoke the drug. He made up his mind that if they were happy to have him, he would return to Hong Kong.

This was of course hard for us to accept, but we wanted the best for him and perhaps this was the best. The next few months were a busy time as he finished his A-levels and worked hard to raise the money for a plane ticket. We all, in our different ways, had to come to terms with the idea of him going away for up to three years. There was one more trip to New Wine that summer as a family, a fantastic farewell barbecue at home with all his many friends, old and young, and at last September arrived, the month of 'mists and mellow fruitfulness'. For me it has always carried a wistful air, as if the elements themselves are aware that it is time now to say goodbye to the fullness of summer and prepare for quieter times. In this gentle and subdued month we faced up to needing to say goodbye to our gentle, rather wistful boy for the time being.

CHAPTER 3

Lessons in Bereavement

Leaving home

Jim sat on my bed, tears pouring down his face. We were within one or two days of his departure for Hong Kong and emotions were running high. He had done very well in his A-levels and, like many of his friends, he could have been preparing to go off to university. Instead, he had emptied his bank account to buy a plane ticket and was planning to give the remainder to the work of St Stephen's. His bag was nearly packed and with tears he informed me that he might never come home. It is really hard to understand this now a few years on. Jim loved his family: that much I know without a doubt. So what was he turning his back on? Perhaps the answer is that he was trying to get away from a part of himself that he found hard to accept. Perhaps, too, he wanted to prove himself in some way. Jim had great admiration for those who, as he saw it, refused to settle for the easier options and took themselves to the edge, testing their faith, courage and endurance. Maybe Jim wanted to be a hero to himself. On top of these factors, of course, Jim was the third child and perhaps he just wanted to make his own mark and do things differently, for now at least. Also, though I wouldn't have dreamt of telling him, I didn't believe for one minute that he would never return to England. At eighteen, life can seem very black and white but we know we see differently as the years pass.

I was crying too. It is so hard to say goodbye to those you love, and the prospect of separation was very painful. Sometimes we have wondered, especially with hindsight, whether we were wrong to let him go to live and work in a drug rehabilitation charity as a rather vulnerable young man, but in truth there wasn't much we could say or do to stop him, even if we had wanted to. It was his money and he was eighteen years old. This was his life and this was what he had chosen. It's also true to say we felt proud of him for his courage and determination to find a way to grow through his problems and to do something so challenging at the same time. We felt he may well be right in his assessment that university would be the wrong place for him for now. It seemed to us that a chance to mature a little could be very positive and perhaps a complete change of environment would be good for him. We were excited for him to be going to a place where Christian faith was lived on the front line too. We were sure that the experience would help him grow as a young man of God. We always remembered those prophetic words given before he was born and believed that maybe this was part of the process by which he would grow into a soldier and servant of Christ.

The first bereavement

It was surreal taking Jim to the airport. There was time to kill before he could check in and we sat in a café, drinking coffee which none of us really wanted, aware of the television above our heads silently screening a soap opera while we lived through our own drama. Trying to make conversation in an almost impossible situation, hearts full to overflowing with unspoken words. Wanting to say how much we loved him, how much he meant to us all, how much he was our beloved child, but knowing how unwelcome any display of emotion would be. Last-minute checks of tickets and passport were made and then the time came for him to pass through passport control: the time to say goodbye.

23

I see him now, rather self-conscious, baggy white tee-shirt, those unflattering long navy shorts to below the knee, black backpack and guitar slung over his slender, still growing shoulders. A final, rather stiff hug, standing in line, casting sheepish looks towards us, and then he was gone, passed through the point where we couldn't join him. It was a kind of relief of course, because it felt too difficult for all of us, trying to do and say the right things when our emotions were running at such high ebb.

Those early months adjusting to life at home without him were really hard for us. Hannah and Tom had already moved away from home, but lived fairly locally, and I could contact them whenever I wanted; this flying of the nest had a very different feeling attached to it. It wasn't just the distance involved but the knowledge that Jim was vulnerable and needed so much love and encouragement which was hard for him to receive. Chloe was now the only child left at home. She and Jim had forged a strong relationship over the past year or two and had become good friends who loved playing the guitar and singing together. There was a huge gap in all our lives. I wandered round the house, doing the chores with tears pouring down my face, telling myself not to be stupid, that he wasn't dead, only in Hong Kong. How ironic that seemed later on. It really was a form of bereavement, in that Jim's leaving represented an ending of one significant part of all of our lives. It is important to realise in writing a book that is primarily about the experience of bereavement, that actually we face endings of different sorts all through our lives, and in some way they are preparation for those final losses that will come to us all at some stage. These ongoing bereavements also need to be allowed for; they may include such significant events as starting school and leaving the security of home, losing a job, loss of health or ending a relationship, and we need to give room to recognising and acknowledging the feelings they will bring up for us. In a very real way, these weeks of learning to live without Jim in our everyday lives acted as a kind of preparation for what was to come, and though I can't say that it made his death any easier to bear, I could clearly remember the feelings I had had at that time.

After he left we had to get used to receiving little or no news from Jim for weeks at a time because it wasn't easy for him to communicate with us. He didn't have access to a mobile phone and there was no computer he could use. When we explained this to friends they were understandably surprised because, after all, Hong Kong is one of the most technologically sophisticated cities in the world. In going to live in a drug rehabilitation community, however, Jim was joining a part of the society that needed to be quite separate from the outside world, as it was necessary for the residents to break off from former relationships and ways of life while they became used to being drug-free. I became a regular letter writer, savouring my special times on Sunday evenings when I would put aside an hour or two and settle down to write to him and fill him in on all the goings-on at home that week. I was determined that he would feel included in family life even though he was 8,000 miles away. We were still his family and we loved him very much indeed.

Jim, however, was eighteen and not really into writing letters on a regular basis. When we did receive a letter, we read it eagerly, looking for clues as to how he 'really was'. Was he all right, was he happy, was he settling down, making friends? All the usual questions parents want answered by their young people who have recently flown the nest.

A new way of life

Jim was discovering the hard way that real life doesn't necessarily have all that much in common with a book where an exciting story over many years is compressed into relatively few pages. The book *Chasing the Dragon*, which meant so much to Jim, was and remains an inspiring story of great faith and obedience to the call of God, and sheer determination, courage and hard work in putting that faith and obedience into practise in a very demanding environment. But naturally it doesn't record the necessity of daily cleaning of floors and toilets, the peeling of endless vegetables and the need to launder clothes for dozens, which are an inevitable part of community life. Where he had expected to live life on the front line of faith, in a dangerous and exciting environment – the stuff of bestselling books – he was instead living in the community house as a helper and taking his part in the routine rotas that kept the community functioning. There were a lot of chores to be done and a lot of time to be filled. This challenge was proving to be stretching in ways he hadn't expected as he discovered that there was no easy escape from the more mundane aspects of life, on either side of the world. On top of this he had more serious issues to face up to as he came to realise that your problems have an unfortunate way of following you wherever you go. His insecurities and uncertainties did not fall away when he boarded the plane. Jim arrived in Hong Kong as he was in England: the same sensitive, questioning, caring and vulnerable young man, but now living out those character-istics in a much more challenging environment, and one where he couldn't escape his feelings by walking the dog, watching a DVD or going out with his mates as he could at home.

There followed times of great emotional confusion for him, painfully laid out in his letters which, once they did arrive, were pages long and written over several days, thus helping him to record both his ups and his downs. They didn't always make easy reading but they were staggeringly honest. That is one of the many things I will always appreciate about Jim – he didn't beat about the bush, he was a real 'call a spade a spade' man. Though he was quiet, if he had something he wanted to say, it was said in a forthright and uncompromising fashion. It would have been so much easier for him simply to write that every-thing was fine and please send his love to the family, but that wasn't his style. Instead we had the pouring out of his heart and sometimes his temper as he tried to adapt to a community life-style with no personal space and no personal time – an environment that would prove highly demanding for anyone. He had tremendous courage, that much is certain, and also many battles to fight with himself, just as he had at home.

After a few months, as he turned nineteen, Jim began to wonder if he had made a mistake in going to Hong Kong. It was painful to hear him through his letters trying to decide what to do. Part of him loved being there with the extraordinary cama-raderie and fellowship. He was learning so much about how other people lived, beginning to understand and speak Canton-ese and using his guitar and music to communicate with men, young and old, who had often experienced very little love or care in their lives. He was also putting his faith on the front line and searching hard for the God he wanted to believe was real but he found difficult to trust. Another part of him, however, felt hemmed in by the close confinement and the lack of freedom to make his own decisions. Community life is never easy. All we could do was reassure him, across the distance, that whatever he did, we would support him and that we truly believed that if he chose to return home, his time there would not have been wasted. As I reflect on these events now, with some hindsight, it is as hard as ever to understand why Jim found it so difficult to find his place in the world. He was loved and respected by many people both in England and Hong Kong, and he also loved and respected many in return. He cared deeply and sometimes I think that was part of the problem – perhaps the pain in the world and the pain in him just seemed too overwhelming.

After much soul-searching Jim elected to remain in Hong Kong and we were able to visit him after he had been there for one year. Jim met us at the airport with a broad smile on his face, and his backpack and guitar slung over his shoulders. He was so pleased to see us, and guide us via an airport bus to our destination, a tiny apartment some twenty floors up in the heart of Kowloon.

It was great to be with him again and to be able to catch up. He was delighted to have a bit more freedom to explore the exciting place in which he had been living for nearly a year. A special treat for him was to watch Liverpool FC playing live on television, usually in the middle of our night. It seemed just like the old days again to hear the familiar commentary and to see him lapping it all up, and I was able to sleep through all the singing, cheering and shouting, just revelling in the sense of being together again. He enjoyed being the one with the local knowledge, chatting away to our cleaning lady in Cantonese, to her great surprise and delight, and proudly guiding us round the city, especially the less salubrious bits.

It soon became clear to us, however, that Jim was still very unsettled and uncertain about what he should do with himself. We stayed for three weeks, and although we had some happy times together there were also hard times as he struggled with deciding what he should do: stay in Hong Kong or return to England? After much deliberation he opted to return to the community home after our short holiday with him, but he was unable to make that decision until the very last moment when we were on the verge of departure for the airport. We watched as he sorted out his bag to return to the community house, disposing of nearly everything, including books and small gifts that we and other friends had given him, retaining just a few items of clothing. Then our taxi arrived and we loaded ourselves and our luggage in and turned round to wave goodbye. Our boy was standing there, on the pavement, with tears flowing down his face while the busy Hong Kong traffic whizzed past, oblivious to the little domestic drama being played out. It all contributed to an anxious homecoming for us.

After a short while we received a letter from him, however, declaring that he felt sure he had made the right decision and he was so pleased he had stayed. He was determined now, he said, to really be part of the place and work hard, to be trusted as a helper and to grow in faith.

The second bereavement

That was what he sincerely meant then, but come December he decided differently again. He arrived back in England just before Christmas, on a very cold and foggy day. We knew, as soon as he walked into the house, that something was wrong. He was home, but clearly unhappy and unsettled. The rest of the family were thrilled to have him with us again, two years and more since he had first left, and we all did our best to welcome him; but a deep unhappiness, and even anger, emanated from him. He said later that the minute he had boarded the plane to leave Hong Kong, he regretted his decision. That came as no surprise to us – we could feel it palpably. Of course, it was hurtful; it just seemed whatever we did was not enough to reassure him or support him. We were constantly crying out for him and holding him before God in our prayers, simply having to believe and trust that all would eventually be all right or otherwise we may have felt despair. Jim would grow up, gain confidence and find his way in a world that didn't seem to have a lot of charm for him right now. We felt, it has to be said, pretty helpless in the face of his sadness and disappointment – with himself or us or God or life, we didn't know.

I often wonder what role cannabis played in all of this emotional lability. Had exposure to that drug in the formative teenage years in some way affected his development and his ways of thinking? Research strongly suggests that cannabis used in adolescence, a critical stage for brain development, can have devastating consequences for some who are genetically vulnerable.[1] He was a young lad of enormous promise and with such a deep desire to live well, and yet there was a power or pressure within him that held him down, and robbed him of any peace of mind.

His few months in England in early 2006 were disastrous for him, that much is clear. I believe now that it was in this time that he grew particularly despondent. He chose to leave Manchester and spend time in London. I will never forget the last time we took him to Manchester Piccadilly station to catch the train south. This was once again an immensely painful separation for us; once again it was bereavement. It was as if he wanted or needed to blank us out – maybe the anguish, whatever caused it, was just too much for him. We had driven away from his childhood home, at one time so much loved by him, and he never even turned for a last look. When we got to the station I tried to hug him and he barely received it. Graeme and I watched him walk away from us to the station entrance. He never once turned round to wave to us. We struggled to hold in our tears long enough to watch him disappear and that was the last time we ever saw him alive – a thin, dejected young man with his back resolutely turned towards us.

When we arrived home soon after and I found the wallet of family photos I had given him to take back with him carelessly cast aside on his bedroom floor, my grief knew no bounds. I howled then, a deep gut-wrenching howl expressive of the deepest soul pain. It was truly another bereavement.

He made friends in London of course, among a loving Christian community. Jim always made friends wherever he went; he reached out to people in their vulnerability and they reached out to him in his. However, there was also a deep loneliness within him, and he and I had long conversations on the phone, him wandering round the streets just talking, talking, talking to me, seemingly almost fearful to put the phone down as he would have to face being alone; and me, pleased with the contact, just trying to 'be there' for him, whatever he needed me to be. He found some casual building work and he found places with friends to sleep, but this was a terrible time. After he died, when we tried to put the pieces of the story together, we believe this is where Jim first got hold of heroin, probably from a homeless person that he was trying to befriend. I am not passing the blame here – Jim was responsible for his decision to accept and use the heroin.

The next weeks were terrible for Jim. We don't know what was going on for him in a detailed way, but eventually he knew that if he was to be saved from his addictive tendencies he needed the help and encouragement of his friends in Hong Kong. He was soon on his way there again and returned to the community house. Unbeknown to us until after his death, he returned this time as an addict in a very poor state of health. Letters written by him to friends and shared with us after his death reveal how ashamed he felt, but also his determination that he was never going to go down the road of addiction again.

He wrote us a very loving letter soon after his return, asking us to send on those abandoned photos, which he claimed he had forgotten – well, maybe he had, in the distress of the moment. He revealed nothing of the poor physical state he was in and I was delighted once again to hear him sounding loving and hopeful.

Good times

Now, at last, there seemed to be a sustained mood of positivity. Jim, aged twenty, was growing up, becoming more mature and surer of what he wanted. In these fifteen or sixteen months, between July 2006 and November 2007, he began to blossom in a remarkable way. His Cantonese language skills had come on well, his music abilities had developed and were used to encourage others and to lead worship; he became a real servant at St Stephen's in many ways. During these months he was able to visit a St Stephen's project in the Philippines which both inspired him greatly and moved him at a very deep level as he witnessed the shocking poverty and inequality. He was also encouraged to branch out a little to the world beyond the community house and he found another role, teaching English to pre-school children whom he quickly grew to love. The staff of that little private school once again, as people did, took him to their hearts and in a short time he became a loved and valued member of their community.

He was looking to his future now and wondering whether at last to return to England to attend university. He had no problem in getting some places offered at good institutions. Meanwhile, while he pondered on his future, he was out on the streets of the city, telling men about Jesus and forming relationships which led some to come into the community house for drug rehabilitation. Several, after his death, affirmed that Jim had been responsible for introducing them to Jesus and for bringing them into an environment where they could be saved – physically and spiritually.

These were good months for Jim, and with each positive email (for now he had more computer access) our spirits soared a little higher for him. It seemed our boy was coming through and growing into the person Jesus had made him to be. We were feeling very happy for him. We were told later by his friends and colleagues that in the last month or two of his life Jim never seemed better – more open, more positive, more hopeful and with a radiant faith in Jesus that made an impact on many who came into contact with him.

In September 2007 we felt strongly that it was high time to go and visit Jim. We were aware of how much he had grown up since we had last seen him in June of the previous year, and we wanted to see this young man for ourselves. It was high time to banish the painful memories of our last parting with some fresh ones. He had already told us he wouldn't be able to come over for Christmas, and when we compared diaries, it seemed best to wait until January, when we might be able to combine our visit with his birthday, and be able to celebrate with him, as we had missed his twenty-first birthday earlier that year. All that now remained was to fix the actual dates so we could book flights and make arrangements to cover our absence in England. After all, those two or three months would soon pass, Christmas would come and go and we would be on our way.

CHAPTER 4

Devastation

The 6th of November 2007 was an ordinary Tuesday and we were both doing ordinary things. It was now just over a year since we had moved to our new home and church in Wirral and it hadn't been an easy fourteen months in many ways. Leaving our friends and church family in Manchester had proved harder than we imagined, our nest was empty for the first time and we missed our children. On top of this I had been badly knocked back by a strange virus that took some time to clear up. I pined for my old way of life and for the job that I had had to give up on moving. It hadn't been easy to find a new direction. Now, however, we had reached a new stage – we were ready to put our roots down and to embrace our new life. I had recently enrolled on a one-year counselling course, as I thought this would be a worthwhile and interesting way of using my abundant spare time until I had found a clear way forward for my future career. Just after that began we took a short holiday – our first on our own in many years – and used some of the time to both look back and look forward and to assess where we had got to. When we returned we were feeling fit, refreshed and ready to offer ourselves and our lives once more to God. After some struggles we had at last reached a good place and were feeling full of energy for the challenges that lay ahead.

That November morning I went to get my hair coloured – a common enough thing to do and yet it was symbolic to me that I had decided to embrace life and look up and out, and the decision to get a full head of highlights felt part of that. The illness of the previous November, on top of our recent house move and all the resulting change, had led to a degree of depression. I was determined this winter it was going to be different and that I was going to live and act positively. I have never found November an easy month, so I felt it was important to be proactive and face it head on. I was particularly pleased with myself as I'd also visited the local Oxfam shop that morning and had picked up a beautiful, richly coloured, pure silk designer jacket for a small price – a real bargain. It seemed like my lucky day. The sun was shining, the autumn colours looked at their glowing best and all felt good with my world on that morning.

Despite my determination to embrace life, however, I was aware of a deeper anxiety. While waiting for the hairdresser to call me, I leafed through the newspaper provided and chanced on an article written about depression in young adults. It resonated with me so much as I thought about Jim and the struggles we had had, that as we ate lunch later I told Graeme about it, and intended to pop up to the newsagents that afternoon to buy my own copy.

The small and unimportant details of this life-changing day stand out remarkably clearly. I remember going home and showing off my new jacket and new hair to Graeme, before making a toastie for lunch.

While we munched we chatted over our morning and talked about possible dates for our forthcoming trip to Hong Kong. We were a bit frustrated because we were waiting for Jim to tell us when it would be most convenient from his end, but somehow that email still hadn't arrived. After a coffee, we separated and each returned to our own tasks.

Shock

Suddenly, soon after we had left the table, Graeme called out for me to come quickly. His tone of voice alerted me to the fact that something was wrong. While we had been eating and discussing our trip, an email had arrived and now I stood behind his chair in his small study reading the words, which though in plain English, barely seemed to make sense. It was from Jackie, who was writing to inform us that Jim was in trouble having been caught with drugs; he had disappeared and no one knew where he was. At one click of a finger, all our plans, our strategies for moving on, our hopes and dreams fell away. We had truly thought that Jim had arrived at a better place within himself, and nothing we had heard or read from him had prepared us for news like this. Everything that felt solid and familiar was swirling around us as we tried to take in information that was beyond us. Everything, even the solid walls of our home, looked and felt different – as if all landmarks had disappeared. It was as if the sun had gone, fog descended and the world had become a strange and dangerous place. We were suddenly plunged into a chaotic world where nothing was as it seemed. It was like falling down a deep hole where before there had been solid land, like Alice falling into wonderland, but at the bottom for us was no wonderland but a kind of hell.

The afternoon passed in a daze as we tried to figure out what we should do. Our first reaction was to book a plane and go to Hong Kong but on phoning St Stephen's we were told to hang on as he could be anywhere – he could even turn up at home. I remember trying to be ordinary – to treat this like any other adolescent misdemeanour and to be angry with his thoughtlessness, but in truth I pretty quickly saw it for what it was and knew from some deep place inside me that there might be the worst of outcomes.

Bizarrely, that evening we went out to a local restaurant with my father who, now frail and elderly, had recently come to live near us. I think some part of us thought that if we just carried on as normal with the things we had planned, then perhaps life would revert to normal again. Poor Dad – we never even told him that anything was wrong, not wanting to worry or upset him when we ourselves knew so little, but instead we just had an almost silent meal, me with my new hair and new jacket virtually choking on every mouthful. Dad, whose senses were dulled in many ways by his poor physical condition, noticed nothing amiss. Looking back, I wonder how I could ever have left the phone in case Jim or someone else phoned. I truly think that in the shock of the event, the balance of our minds was disturbed – to go out and leave the phone was a kind of madness or at least a kind of denial that anything was really wrong.

I do remember coming home and phoning Jim's godparents and asking them to pray, however, and then lying in a kind of agony on the sofa until eventually we went to bed. A telephone call from Jackie at 11.35 pm, our time, gave us the news we most feared. Jim had been found dead, in a flat in a downtown area of Hong Kong. The cause of death was unknown, but drug use was suspected. In Hong Kong the date of his death was recorded as 7th November, but in England it was still 6th November, so strangely, we have two dates on which he died.

Many before us have walked the road of sudden traumatic bereavement and many have walked it since, and I'm sure anyone who has been there knows that it is almost impossible to put into words how it feels when you get news like that in the middle of the night – or any other time of day, I suppose. Is there even any value in trying to put into words something so terrible, so visceral? I am not sure really, but maybe the unbearable has to be borne in words as well as in real life, so that others who want to support friends or family members may understand as far as possible why it is that it takes for ever for life to be normal again and why those so affected may truly believe for a while that they will never smile again. There are, of course, many metaphors to describe the indescribable, and all metaphors only go so far. Having said this, the best I can come up with is having a limb ripped off or an organ ripped out. 'Amputation' is too tidy, a word that carries images of clinical operating theatres and anaesthesia, and there was nothing clinical about this.

On that terrible night a force ripped me from my bed like electricity and I found myself howling like an injured animal on the other side of my room. I have since watched many screen depictions of sudden grief and think that maybe this is not an unusual experience, though at the time it felt violent and frightening. I remember lying awake the rest of the night, with a familiar ache in the pit of my stomach – a feeling that I recalled from giving birth: I was now empty, my baby had gone from me. I lay quietly in the dark, dreading morning coming because then we would need to draw the curtains and what felt too awful to be real would become real. I felt that when the curtains were opened we would be like actors walking onto a stage playing our roles, because this terrible thing couldn't be real – surely we were just play-acting? It was like walking on to the set of countless television dramas that I had watched over the years. But of course there had been no rehearsal for anything like this in our lives, there was no stage make-up or costumes to hide behind. We had no choice but to stumble onto the stage and in some ways improvise our roles as newly grieving parents until the reality of our situation had sunk in.

It is strange how, when your own world stops, nothing else does. Before we knew it, daylight broke, the milkman called and the dog had to be let out. The sounds of a new morning as people made their way to school or work gradually gathered momentum. So far, no one else knew in England . . . it was our own private secret and it felt a bit better that way. But reality broke in and suddenly we found ourselves calculating that if it was 7 am in England it wouldn't be too long before offices closed in Hong Kong. There were so many people we needed to contact – the British Consul and Hong Kong undertakers among others. How surreal life felt, compared to the familiar world of hairdressing appointments and toasted sandwiches, less than 24 hours before.

So many things come to mind as I write . . . at least I had a good and loving husband beside me to go through this with, at least I had other children, at least it was only one of my children – not all of them, as too many parents in many parts of the world have to endure. All of these things are true and I thank God for them, but just as you love each child 100 per cent, so you feel the loss of one, 100 per cent. The loss of a child is a searing pain that burns through to your very core.

A while after Jim died, I wrote in my journal that sudden loss or trauma is like an earthquake which leads to devastation. The landscape of your life is changed for ever as one significant part of it is ripped away, and the task you are left with is to learn to negotiate the land again where nothing looks or feels the same. I posed the question then, 'How are you to do this – living in the same country but with your familiar landmarks gone, your old securities and your old way of seeing and being, gone?'

I wrote a poem a few months later as I reflected on an observation made to me that I hadn't been the same since Jim had died. It attempts to capture the almost physical nature of the pain and anguish:

I am changed for ever
Do you know what it feels like when your leg is ripped away with no anaesthetic?
Nor do I, but I know what it felt like when someone I loved with all my heart was ripped away.
It felt as if my heart was torn apart with no anaesthetic.
It really hurt and it left a big gaping dripping bleeding hole
Which can never ever be healed.

Oh yes, maybe some scar tissue will form,
The bleeding will stop.
But do you know what scar tissue is like?
It is hard and inflexible and it pulls and is tight.
It can even stick to other parts of you,
Turn normal you into damaged you.
And it is so there,
Different colour, different feel, different look
Not the same as the 'you' that was there before.
It covers up the wound,
It helps you to go from day to day,
Doing the ordinary everyday things.
But, you are right,
I am changed for ever.

I remember Easter, some eighteen months after Jim had died. I was in church on Good Friday listening to the Scriptures and trying to understand the pain God felt on seeing his son die. My imagination couldn't get there, and then suddenly it felt as if God said to me, 'In the depth of your own pain and the depth of your own love, as you grieve for your lost son, I have helped you to understand how much love I feel and how much pain I feel'. Just a glimpse, just a little, I understand 'poured out love' and 'anguish of the soul' . . . the sort of anguish that made Jesus sweat gouts of blood.

Unreal reality

As that new morning dawned, we continued to be torn between knowing that this devastation was real and life changing and yet acting as if it wasn't such a big deal. Graeme, like many new vicars, had spent his first year in the parish surveying the scene and trying to get a measure of understanding of how this new place ticked. A parish is rather like a family, I think . . . though there may be many things in common, each one is unique with its own history and its own culture. It takes time to get a handle on these things. He had planned an open evening meeting that very night, 7th November 2007, to discuss the future vision of the church, to try and gauge what people were hoping for and where God might be taking us. Believe it or not, we lay in bed that morning with a cup of tea, discussing whether Graeme might still be able to lead the meeting that evening, before attending to all the things that were now waiting for us. It just seems crazy now and we soon saw it for a kind of craziness then, but as I said before, trauma like this stops you thinking properly. Thankfully some kind of sense reasserted itself, and we knew that the first thing we had to do was cancel any arrangements we had made for the next few days and weeks.

There were still obligations we couldn't escape, however – I had arranged to take my father to the doctor that morning, first thing. I did so, sitting with him in the waiting-room full of snuffles and sneezes, nursing the worst of secrets in my breast. I didn't know how I was going to tell this sick old man that his 21-year-old grandson had just died from unknown causes and we were going to have to leave him to fly to Hong Kong as soon as possible. Then, of course, there were the other children scattered at this point round the north-west of England – how were we to tell them this terrible news?

The next two or three days were a flurry of trips across to Manchester and over the Pennines to Sheffield, doing the best we could as a family to support one another in this most unexpected of crises. In between the driving, making sure my father was cared for, sorting out the dog and the cat, packing our bags for a long-haul trip and informing as many of our friends as we could – and, most painful of all, dealing with an invasive press – we managed to book plane tickets, with the help of our friends in Hong Kong. They were so good to us in these awful days and did all they could.

The questioning begins

Where was God in all this? Did he know and did he care, this God to whom we had been praying about Jim for over 22 years? Had he heard any of those prayers, or had we got it wrong all the way through; not prayed well enough or not been faithful enough? How could our beautiful son, who had so much potential and who was so well loved by many people, end up dying tragically in downtown Hong Kong, far, far away from the family who loved him? How did it end up like this? There was one question shouting at me that may as well have been written in big black letters on the wall of our house: 'What did we do wrong?' Any parents in such a situation are bound to ask themselves such things – and it is very painful, especially once you know there is no way back; the worst has happened and there is no glimmer of hope that things will turn out all right in the end if you just stick with it.

So, the question remains: where was God? I think he was there with us in all sorts of subtle and not so subtle ways, shown through the extraordinary kindness of men and women. How can I forget the roasted chicken, in its special foil bag, pushed through the cat-flap by someone who just wanted to say they cared about us? Even at the time it made us chuckle to find the chicken lying there . . . we were so moved by the gesture and we knew that it was a wordless expression of love. That chicken meant a lot to us, though I can't remember if we or the cat ate it in the end. It was a terrible time for us, it is true – and it wasn't so good for the chicken either! Perhaps it seems tasteless to smile at such a time or even when writing about it some years later, but actually, laughter is also God's gift to us, as much as tears. Jim laughed a lot, and we laughed together a lot. We knew he too would have chuckled at this . . . in our humour we were close to him, just as we were in our grief.

I believe that God made himself known to us in a more

overt way too. Two days after Jim died, our local Bishop and good friend, Keith Sinclair, visited us. We sat at our kitchen table together in a kind of mutual desolation and I remember saying, 'I just need to know that God is with us in this, I need a sign.' Later that morning Graeme received a phone call from another dear friend who worked in a high-pressured environment in the City. Richard had felt compelled to leave a business meeting to phone us there and then. He didn't want to talk as such, but he felt he had some words that he needed to pass on and which couldn't wait as they were burning in him: 'Jim is a soldier of the Lord, he has fallen in battle and he is with Jesus'. He repeated this message with some urgency several times, and when Graeme responded with a grateful but bemused thank you, he repeated it again, saying, 'No, I don't think you understand, Jim is a soldier of the Lord, he has fallen in battle and he is with Jesus'. Some time after, when we spoke to Richard about this, he told us he felt he had no choice but to phone then and pass it on. This was the more remarkable in that Richard, who is a very godly man and a true prayer warrior, was not generally given to a ministry of prophetic words. Neither did he know about the prophecy given to us before Jim was born, and that we had prayed regularly for him ever since, that he would be a soldier and servant of the Lord.

I felt that this was the sign I had asked for that we would know that God was indeed with us in this. It is not possible to express how much that helped us in the dark weeks and months that were to follow. It was as if hope and trust were there, running parallel with grief and desolation. Of course it answers none of the questions of 'Why?' but we know there are no answers to such questions. That does not make it wrong to ask them – they are the inevitable cry of a human soul in pain.

In those terrible days before arriving in Hong Kong, there were many occasions for tears, laughter and gratitude. The tears just were and need no explanation. The laughter was released again when we found ourselves staying in surely the worst bed and breakfast in Sheffield (or possibly England), where we went to see Chloe, our youngest daughter. Whereas normally I think I would have felt rather cross, somehow in extremis I could see how ridiculous it all was, even down to the used dental floss stick lying on our bed, the ragged, grubby-looking towels, the unlabelled bathroom that led to Graeme walking into someone else's bedroom in the small hours, and the cutlery that was stuck, gungily, to the table! Along with the forlorn, abandoned chicken on our doormat, I could not help seeing the funny side. I suppose that was an effect of heightened emotions and, beyond this, I suspect laughter must be a gift we have to help us survive.

The gratitude flowed in many ways as we received so many messages of love and support and some unexpected blessings. Chloe, our youngest, showed her love and pride in her brother by somehow finding the courage, less than 48 hours after hearing of his death, to play some of his favourite songs on her guitar in his honour at an open mike session in a local Sheffield pub, and was given a warm reception. Other friends, who also knew the pain of losing a child, gave us a money gift, knowing the many expenses that accrue at such a time. We were able to spend some of this on buying a video camera which we used to record the memorial service held one week later in Hong Kong. Once home we were able to share it with our family and friends and it has been a real comfort to all of us.

Ready for departure

The night before we were due to leave for Hong Kong, we had done all we could to get ready and had retired to bed in nervous anticipation of the long trip and difficult situation we had to face once there. Suddenly, shortly before midnight, there was a loud and insistent ringing of our doorbell and the sound of thumping on the door. Graeme ran downstairs, adrenalin pumping hard, both of us immediately full of dread at who this may be, bothering us so insistently at this time. But there was also another thought instantly in both our minds – had it all been a ghastly mistake and Jim wasn't dead and had found his way home?

The solution was more mundane of course. An ambulance team on their way to an emergency had got lost and come to the wrong house. Terrible for them, worse for whoever it was facing an emergency, but also shocking for us. Such a thing had never happened before or since, and it seemed so strange that it should happen on that night, of all nights. Our minds, so recently and deeply traumatised, could hardly contain the unreality of all that was happening around us.

Finally, three and a half days after the news of Jim's death, we boarded the plane to fly to Hong Kong, not knowing what awaited us there or what kind of reception we would face. We didn't know exactly what Jim had done, or how his friends and colleagues felt about him. After all, he had gone there to help others and had now died himself possibly of the very thing the charity was seeking to release men and women from. I was afraid that perhaps he was perceived as some sort of failure and disgrace. So there was much that was still unknown, and we felt a great deal of trepidation. How amazing then, the grace of God, that we should, through the help of St Stephen's, find ourselves flying with a Christian airline, now sadly no longer functioning, as, like so many others, they hit hard times in the recession of 2008. How amazing that as we waited for take-off, the music playing should be worship songs we were familiar with. At that time they were like balm to our battered souls, especially when an instrumental version of Tim Hughes's song, 'May the Words of My Mouth' began to play. I had given Jim the words of this song when he finally left us back in June 2006 to return to London and then Hong Kong. I had written on the back of the piece of paper that these words seemed to me to sum up what Jim was trying to do, and that I would be praying for him in this way. I remember Jim had looked doubtful but he took the paper with the words on anyway, and when we got to look through his few possessions some days after he died, I found he had kept them safely, as if he treasured them. They are as follows:

May the words of my mouth and the thoughts of my heart
Bless Your name, bless Your name, Jesus
And the deeds of the day and the truth in my ways
Speak of You, speak of You, Jesus
For this is what I'm glad to do
It's time to live a life of love that pleases You
And I will give my all to You
Surrender everything I have and follow You
I'll follow You

Lord, will You be my vision, Lord, will You be my guide
Be my hope, be my light and the way
And I'll look not for riches, nor praises on earth
Only You'll be the first of my heart

I will follow
I will follow
I will follow You[1]

Jim, in his own way, had been trying to follow God and had given up everything in his pursuit. He wasn't particularly spiritually strong or wise, but he was, if nothing else, sincere and courageous, and a flavour of that is caught in the words of the song. For me, it is truly a 'Jim song'.

Such unexpected blessings told me that surely, in all the mess and in all the heartbreak, God was still with us and cared deeply for Jim. In no way did this lessen the fearful blow of losing Jim, but there was consolation to be found in hanging on to the belief that we were not on our own, however desperate it felt.

CHAPTER 5

Searching Through the Rubble

Travelling to Hong Kong at this time just felt something we needed to do, though it was very difficult to leave our other children who were reeling, as we were. We needed to be with Jim's friends and, as his Mum and Dad, we wanted to be with him and let him know he wasn't on his own. We had many questions to ask, though we were not sure how many of them could be answered – what happened, how did it happen, why did it happen? Maybe the most painful one was to discover whether Jim's involvement with drugs had gone so far as to betray the charity he was working with . . . had he actually peddled drugs to those he was meant to be helping? There were other questions too. Was his death suicide? Could something have been done to prevent it?

As I reflect on those days, I find myself living with the paradox that though losing Jim was so deeply terrible, we have, in his loss, been richly blessed by the love we have been shown and by the discoveries we made about our very ordinary son – that is to say, ordinary like the rest of us. As I write, I am aware that it would do Jim a great disservice to try and make him anything other than what he was: a sensitive, caring and loving young man, beset with his own deep soul pain, for reasons we can never understand. I am also aware that we have been able to receive a great deal of consolation through being able to visit his friends, and share, cry and laugh together about our memories.

I know that some bereaved parents and families may never be in a position to receive such consolation and I find it hard to imagine the additional pain that might cause. I hope my recollections will not exacerbate anyone else's grief, but instead help us to remember how each person who becomes addicted to drugs in some way, and maybe loses their life to those drugs, is an individual, loved by many and with their own story.

During those few days we were accommodated in a flat in the complex where Jim had been living until his death. The flats were available either for female helpers in the community, or for married couples who came to stay with the community, for varying lengths of time to offer help in any way they could. How poignant it was for us to discover that just a week or so before his death, Jim had been cleaning that flat with another young English man, Tim, who was also working there. Tim told us how, as they cleaned together, Jim had commented that one day he hoped to be married and come back with his wife to Hong Kong to maybe stay in that flat, and help other young people as he had been helped. How ironic that the next people to take advantage of the newly cleaned flat were his own parents. But even in that rather sad story there was some comfort to be found, because we heard that Jim was looking to the future and appreciative of the kindness he himself had been shown.

The flat was lovely: small, clean and bright with long views into the hills on the other side of the valley. In the valley lay the new territories town of Shatin, once a sleepy fishing port but over the past two or three decades grown out of all recognition. It was now a bustling town some distance from the central hub of Hong Kong and probably most famous for its race course and equestrian centre, where events were held for the 2008 Beijing Olympics. We were moved to find a box of English-style groceries ready for us on our arrival including tea, bread and cereal. Usually, we are keen to try whatever a new culture has to offer, but this was a time for home comfort as far as possible. A large vase of oriental pink lilies graced the small table in the living-room and filled the space with their powerful scent. Now I often have a similar bunch of lilies in my own hallway as a way of linking with Jim and his friends in Hong Kong. Until losing Jim I don't think I'd ever bought flowers for myself and it is a small extravagance to be sure, but one thing I have learnt in the years since is that if something like this can bring some comfort, then it is worth doing.

Painful practicalities

After any death there are many tasks that have to be completed, even though they are the last things you feel capable of doing at that time. When the death happens unexpectedly and over-seas, procedures that are already hard seem to become almost unbearable. The day after we arrived we had to go to the under-taker to view Jim's body and to discuss plans for returning him to England. This of course was never going to be easy, but it was made even more difficult in an unfamiliar culture. We found the surroundings very different from those of an undertaker at home, and it was, truly, an alien environment in many ways. We found ourselves in a huge emporium built on many levels which looked like any large office building. We walked down long corridors past many Buddhist side chapels where ceremonies were in progress, before we got to the room where Jim was, to begin the process of saying goodbye to him. We were grateful that Jackie came with us to guide us through a very difficult experience and to pray for us throughout. Sadly, through her work with addicts she was no stranger to the place.

We also had to arrange for practical things like money transfer from our accounts in England so that expenses could be covered. Before the undertaker would do any more for us, he needed to be paid. I naïvely thought that in this global, 24/7 society it wouldn't be difficult to move money around the world, but I was wrong. Many hours were spent sitting in an HSBC bank in Kowloon trying to get the problem sorted out. It is hard now to describe the peculiar agony of having to deal with such needless and tangled bureaucratic nonsense in front of the polite, kindly but nevertheless rather hopeless young bank employees, when inside you were crying out in such deep soul pain. I suppose it is the utter unreality of such a situation that gets you through in some way. It is hard to believe that what is happening is true, so you just go along with it, like an actor in a play. In the end we were saved by some new friends in Hong Kong who lent us a large sum of money temporarily so that we could pay our bills without causing any more delay.

More difficulty ensued when we tried to shut Jim's bank account, something we needed to do for the simple reason that we knew we would find it painful to keep receiving bank statements for him once we were home. It seemed no one was able to believe we really were his parents and therefore had the authority to do this. Jim had only £78 in the account . . . we were tickled in a way that there was considered to be any likelihood we might be some sort of international tricksters who had flown almost around the world to enrich ourselves with less than £80. But 'rules are rules' and nobody was going to risk contravening them, even when common sense was being seriously challenged. Trying to get through the bureaucracy took us two or three long, tiring days, leading us to becoming better acquainted with the Hong Kong subway system than we ever expected to be as we trekked from government office to government office. At one point it was even suggested we might like to fly our solicitor to Hong Kong to verify we were who we said we were. Really there are no words to express how this made us feel! In the end we got through this by casting ourselves on the mercy of the British consul and pleading for them to help us. Finally we were given extra documentation that verified we were who we said were, and so at last, after many hot tears of frustration and despair had rolled down both our weary faces, we found ourselves in possession of Jim's tiny inheritance. It helped pay for the taxi and subway fares that we had run up over the past three days, at least.

Worst of all, perhaps, was the depressing visit to the grey police station to collect the few belongings found with Jim after he died. It's not that the officials were unkind or unfeeling, but this was just a job to them, and Jim was just another young expat who had probably overindulged. The officer put Jim's tatty old backpack on the table and proceeded to check off the contents with us, one by one. There wasn't much there and it didn't take long, but we were deeply moved to find among his few items of clothing the latest batch of family photos I had sent out a few weeks before. If we needed it – and at that time we did – this was proof that, to the last, Jim had cared about his family enough to grab a few pictures of us all when he was *in extremis*.

Finding out about our boy

These were raw, exceedingly painful days, and yet thankfully at the same time we also received a lot of comfort. Otherwise, the utter bleakness of our tasks may have overcome us. We became like private investigators, searching through the evidence, trying as far as we could to discover what had been going on in Jim's life that had led to his desperate death in that sad flat. We talked to anyone and everyone who could tell us about Jim's life in those last months, and so bit by bit we were able to piece together a portrait of the young man. It became like trying to complete a jigsaw – we would find one piece of information, and then another, until we almost had a full picture. We knew that some pieces of that jigsaw would always be missing as no one can really say with certainty what is happening inside another person, and we knew that was something we would have to get used to living with. By the time we returned home, however, some ten days later, we had learnt so much, and in the months to come we continued to add to this picture, as people we didn't know but who knew Jim, contacted us. In all of this we really felt the goodness and grace of God. Through talking to Jim's friends, through letters we were subsequently sent and through the pages of his own rather disjointed diaries and reflections, we were able to discover a great deal that encouraged us, and while nothing could make up for his loss, there was comfort to be found in our discoveries. Importantly, in answer to some of the anxieties we had travelled out with, we learnt that Jim had not involved others in his drug-taking and thus betrayed St Stephen's, and also that he had had plans for his future, so it felt right to infer that his death was accidental, not planned.

A memorial service was held seven days after his death in the beautiful setting of the garden created in memory of Jackie's husband who had died a few years before. The sun was shining brightly down on us as around 200 men and women gathered to pray, worship and share memories of Jim. I think he would have felt overwhelmed at what was said then; we certainly were. We knew that Jim was lovable, but nothing had prepared us for the way so many others obviously did as well. As friends and colleagues, they had got to see different facets of Jim that were hidden from us as his parents. Now we got to hear about the young man who had grown so much over the last year or so, and had been enabled to come alongside men and boys who few others were able to reach. We heard about the young man who had grown into leading worship in a liberated way that lifted his heart and the hearts of his fellow worshippers – the young man who, in his last few weeks, according to those near him, radiated a tremendous sense of love and joy. Or again, the young man who became known for volunteering for extra night duties, sitting and praying with addicts going through the pains of withdrawal, or extra cleaning chores, when few others wanted or felt able to do them. Many of the recovering addicts who gathered that day told, through tears, of how Jim had reached them, just by being with them, not needing to say anything or do anything, but just valuing them for who they were, despite everything. One man expressed it thus, 'He was in between, he understood two worlds and was a bridge. He recognised and understood wisdom, like an old man in a young man's body'. Yet another man testified how 'he was one of the very few who could get alongside our son'. We heard about how the warmth of his smile touched people, how he would leave a game of football just to walk and walk round the pitch and listen to one of the other helpers who was struggling. We heard how he had built relationships with many and brought them into the healing environment of St Stephen's and how, in his last months, he had ventured outside St Stephen's to volunteer as an English teacher in a nursery class. He loved that work, quickly became part of the team and, as he discovered that he enjoyed teaching, wondered whether it might be pointing him towards a future direction for his life.

I am a mother and, like any mother, love to hear good things about my children, but I must admit I was taken aback by the volume of love, affection and respect given to him. I wondered if it was 'just because he had died' that people were saying such warm things, but we found for months and even two or three years after his death, we continued to be told similar testimonies of how he had loved and helped many people, through the love of Christ which was at work in him. One letter from a person we had never met, said that in his 21 years, Jim had done more than many of us achieve in a lifetime, and as I listened to and read many stories about him, I certainly felt that Jim had indeed achieved more than I have, in my longer life.

Yet more uncomfortable questions

Needless to say, such accolades warmed our hearts and made us feel proud of our funny, droll, shy, rather awkward boy; and yet, of course, there were many things we were still unable to understand. Especially, of course, if he was doing so well, why did it all end so badly?

Earlier I mentioned the paradox of how we could receive so much solace in the midst of so much pain, and here is another paradox. Jim was growing up, literally and spiritually. He had grown into a strong, vibrant faith and was being enabled to reach out to and help many people. But in the midst of his spiritual growth he was still a vulnerable young man who had his own battles to fight. The emotional and spiritual frailty that he had recognised within himself and had caused him to go to Hong Kong in the first place was still a part of him. There was still a real battle to be fought. I remember on one day during our stay in St Stephen's I commented to Jackie that I felt angry but didn't know where to put my anger as I didn't want to feel angry with Jim. She replied, wisely, that it was right to be angry and the anger needed to be directed at the enemy – the devil. We are, after all, told 'the devil prowls around like a lion looking for someone to devour' (1 Peter 5.8). In all my reflecting since, this is the answer that makes most sense to me. I believe we are in a spiritual battle. Paul tells us in no uncertain terms that there are 'spiritual forces of evil in the heavenly places' (Ephesians 6.12). Jim was in a battle and there is no question that he was on the front line, in a place like St Stephen's. As he helped many, seeing them find release from their addictions and coming to faith in Jesus, spiritual forces gathered around him. Jim, aged 21, living in a challenging and difficult environment, and carrying his own vulnerabilities, was overwhelmed and fell in battle. I know it is contentious to write like this, but it is hard to see things differently from our perspective, especially in the context of the prophecies given before his birth and just after his death.

Saying this is not the same as saying I believe the devil is a cloven-hoofed figure with horns on his head. Whoever or whatever the devil is, I think the issue is a great deal more complex than that and, while it can be convenient for those agnostic about the Christian faith to snigger and accuse us of having a medieval belief system, if the devil is reduced to such a semi-comical, kind of make-believe figure, we overlook the real spiritual dangers that are lurking around us all, believers or otherwise. Eugene Peterson writes of the devil as 'the malignant will that tempts and seduces us away from the will of God. We have to contend with all of that. We are in a battle. There is a fight of faith to be waged.'[1]

Of course it would also be possible to disregard any spiritual explanation and simply say that, though Jim was a good-hearted person, the lure of drugs on his life was just too strong for him, and that doesn't make him bad, just wounded. No doubt there is truth in this too. One thing is certain – drugs, especially heroin, exert power over the lives of many who dabble with them. It is an especially dangerous power because at first the user may retain the illusion of being in control.

Trying to answer one question always gives rise to the next one: 'Where was Jesus in all of this? Isn't his power greater than the devil's, or the power of heroin? Couldn't he have healed Jim from his weakness?' After all, lots of people were praying for him. I struggled greatly with this, of course, and had times of shouting at God, angry at how I felt that Jim had been let down by him. For some time, I wondered whether my faith was actually empty and I had been kidding myself all these years. My response now, formed in the furnace of great pain, is that we are all in a battle, and all battles have casualties on both the winning and the losing sides. Jim, as a follower of Christ, is on the winning side, and he is a casualty of the battle that rages, unseen, around us. This isn't meant in any way to tidy the situation up or provide bite-size answers to questions of suffering. In no way am I capable of that, but nevertheless, I have had to try to get my mind round the fact of Jim's death, and while I can't find answers, perhaps I can find a few clues that have at least helped me a little. Our immense personal pain on losing him remained and had to and has to be lived through. Any attempt to sweeten the pill and provide simplistic answers are no help at all when dealing with deep pain, and this is not what I am trying to do here. If anything, perhaps a better response is to decide to recognise the battle that is raging unseen and to do all we can to be alert to the spiritual realities. As a Christian, I believe we live in the times between Christ's resurrection and the coming of the kingdom of heaven when Christ returns in glory. So while we will see God act in miraculous ways from time to time, we will also experience much conflict in this world on a personal and global scale. Jim lived among many men and women who could testify that they had been set free from their addictions as they had turned to Christ, but, for some reason we can't understand, that was not Jim's story.

Meanwhile, as parents, brothers and sisters and friends we are bereft, as are many others, of a loved son and brother who meant and means so much to us, and in that situation we have to decide how we are to respond.

Amazing grace

In the midst of pain there is so much unexpected grace. As I previously mentioned, we hadn't long lived in our new home and were still actively working on building new relationships in our church and community. There was one couple linked to the congregation we had had a little contact with in the year or so prior to Jim's death. Heather was English, and Wing On was from Hong Kong, and at this point they still lived in Hong Kong, although they visited England from time to time. On one of those occasions we were delighted to meet them and discover our common interests. We soon discovered that their daughter and her fiancé worked with St Stephen's as Jim did. That was coincidental enough, but the coincidence took on even greater proportions when we found out that in fact their soon-to-be son-in-law was now Jim's team leader and that they were sharing a flat and working out on the streets together for some months of the year that Jim died. Once back in Hong Kong, Heather emailed me once or twice to say she had seen Jim and he looked well. He had even been part of a group that helped her and Wing On move house from one part of Hong Kong to another, and Heather had sent me a photo of him hard at work, shifting furniture.

After his death and during our days in Hong Kong, the presence of Heather and Wing On was such a balm to us, as they, knowing the local system, smoothed the way for some of the bureaucracy and simply extended love and support. To know that there were two people who were linked with both home and Hong Kong and who understood first-hand about the kind of work Jim had been doing was powerful and comforting for us. But best of all, they provided us with an English picnic – cheese sandwiches and cake and apples – when we needed ordinary, familiar things. Sometimes the smallest things can seem like the greatest gifts, and I will never forget that. In the midst of what felt like chaos to us, it seemed God had reached in through two ordinary people to say that we weren't forgotten. It was truly a sign of grace.

Back to England

Once we were sure we had done all we could in talking to Jim's friends and getting a picture of what had been happening for him in the weeks and months before he died, and we knew that Jim's body was safely returned to England, we too were able to return.

Nearly three weeks after his death, Jim's funeral was held in the church where he had grown up between the ages of four and eighteen and where he was known and loved. We were overwhelmed, once again, with the amount of love shown to Jim and the rest of our family, as hundreds attended, many travelling long distances to be there. Graeme, Tom, and Andy our son-in-law took their places as pall-bearers – a terrible job for any father and brothers. Later I wrote a poem that tried to capture the exquisite pain of those moments for a bereaved father:

Two short years ago, an infinite amount of sorrow ago
He carried you then, my love,
For the last time.
Strong shoulders but bowed under your weight –
Your dear self
But also the weight of grief.
Proud to bear you
Not wanting to trust you to anyone else
But the heaviest load he had ever borne.
Holding you high
But also having to let you go
From his fatherly embrace
To the embrace of your God.

Graeme preached again, as he had at the memorial service in Hong Kong. I was so proud of him, as he spoke with great clarity about Jim and his faith in God. Among Jim's possessions we had found his rather scratchy journals where he had recorded with great honesty many of his struggles. Here we found Jim's own testimony; he had written out in full the words of Jesus, 'I am the resurrection and the life. Those who believe in me, even though they die, will live and everyone who lives and believes in me will never die. Do you believe this?' Jim had then written, 'On earth I am the same, I will die. But I WILL (his capitals) rise from the dead. I BELIEVE this. Don't forget it.'

The large Victorian church was packed on the day. I was amazed by that, and I remember hugging so many people who just wanted to express their love, though I confess that in the emotion, the faces of those who attended have become blurred to me. Many were people I knew and loved, but others were strangers to us who loved Jim. Love was tangibly present that day, and that helped to sustain us in the weeks to come. All in all, I think Jim, a private young man, would have been very embarrassed at the outpouring.

Three long weeks

I look back wryly as I remember how positive I felt when I had set out for the hairdresser three long weeks ago, on what I thought was an ordinary Tuesday. I recall how I came home feeling very pleased with myself and with my purchases on that sunny lunchtime. How ironic it seems that what was meant to be symbolic of my determination to make a fresh start became instead 'mourning weeds' worn to Jim's funeral. I already had what I needed for that terrible day. It seemed to me that in some mysterious way I cannot understand, God knew that it was no ordinary Tuesday and that he had helped me, unwittingly, to prepare. Perhaps this is fanciful, but it helped me a little at the time, and it still does. The words of Psalm 23 remain as relevant as ever:

Even though I walk through the valley of the shadow of death, I fear no evil; for you are with me.

CHAPTER 6

Aftershocks

We'll never be six again – a bereaved family

It is in the dark days and weeks after a funeral that the new and painful reality of your life really hits. Somehow it is possible to keep going up to that time. There are so many things to put your mind to and, if you are fortunate, there is a great deal of support around you, to help you through the process that eventually you get to and make it through that terrible day. Afterwards though, it is different. Suddenly the funeral, the focus of so much energy, is over, other people are inevitably busy and need to get on with their own lives, and the bereaved can find themselves terribly adrift with their loneliness and despair. Now life can feel really bleak, as you grapple with your personal earthquake and try to make sense of how you are going to carry on. It can be tempting to wonder if it is worth carrying on, or even if it is possible. These are the times when the bereaved really need support and care from those around them.

For us as a family these were remarkably testing days. We wanted to be there for each other at a time when we were all totally broken and empty. We each had our own relationship with Jim, and though we had in common losing a family member, we had also lost a personal relationship that was unique. There was going to be no easy way through the pain that lay ahead.

It seemed as if the shape of our family had changed for ever.

Where there had been six of us, there were now five, and we all had to adapt to what that meant. It felt lopsided and out of shape, clumsy and uncomfortable for all of us. Tom had shared a room with Jim for eighteen years, and now his best friend, sparring partner and football rival (Jim had stubbornly supported Liverpool FC, while Tom was for Manchester United) was gone. Hannah, his elder sister, had been nurturing and enjoying a new and deepening relationship with Jim now that he was growing beyond his adolescent years and communicating more freely and frequently. Chloe had looked up to and admired Jim, formed a close friendship with him in the last two or three years together at home, and felt very much the youngest with the bigger gap between herself and the others. For each one the loss was huge and irreparable – their memories of their childhood, the family videos and all those silly family stories we collect over the years would never be the same. As their parents, we felt this acutely for them. We were also aware of the danger of idolising Jim in a way that would cause them to feel they could never measure up to this dead son of ours. We knew it was important to remember Jim as he was, full of strengths and weaknesses, rather than recreate him as our 'lost wonder boy'.

We quickly recognised it is not easy to be a bereaved sibling. They found themselves fielding many kind and concerned questions as to how we, the parents, were doing while they were feeling deeply bereaved themselves. It sometimes felt to them as if the immensity of their own loss was not being fully recognised. I write this not by way of grumbling, but merely to highlight the needs of a whole family when one member is lost. It is just very hard for the family and for anyone around them at such a difficult time. Everyone tries their best, but in times of great sensitivity I suppose it is inevitable that feelings get hurt along the way. I guess too that in the awkwardness that bereavement can bring to those who want to show concern, it may feel easier to deflect that a little by asking about how someone else was doing, rather than the person who is in front of you. I myself know that I have often found it difficult to know what to say to the recently bereaved and have only begun to learn through personal experience.

Bereaved parents

The death of a child is horribly painful. 'For most people, the greatest loss to bear is the death of a child', writes one well-known psychotherapist.[1] Another specialist in the field says, 'It really does hurt as bad as they (the parents) say . . . And there is nothing we can do to make it better.'[2] And those are the experts!

For parents, the loss of a child at any age or stage is a terribly traumatic experience and it can place a terrible strain on a relationship, even one that has been previously strong. Grief is a personal process, unique to each person who has to deal with it, and while many of our feelings are shared and we have mutual loss as parents who created and nurtured a child, we also need to respond in our own ways. These can be terrible days, as each partner may find they grieve differently. It is a time when accusations can begin to fly around:

'How can you go back to work so quickly? Don't you care about what has happened?'

'You never seem to cry. I don't think you feel it as much as I do', or perhaps, 'He cries much more than I do . . . what's wrong with me? Maybe I just don't feel enough.'

It may be that one person has a need to talk at length about what has happened, while the other finds it unbearably painful and prefers to keep silent. Disrupted sleep patterns, problems with eating, or recourse to drugs or excessive alcohol in an attempt to mask the pain might all exacerbate a difficult situation. Partners may find that their sexual lives are affected as they react to loss on every level – physically, emotionally and spiritually. Many will find that they need external support to help them understand why they are struggling so much, while others will prefer to go it alone, and, for better or worse, find their own solutions. This is a time when each partner needs to treat the other with great gentleness, and it isn't easy when both are in deep pain.

For Graeme and I the days were bleak indeed in that first winter. The demands on each of us seemed endless and we survived in a fog of exhaustion and what felt dangerously close to despair. We simply didn't know how to do this; how to travel on this steep and rocky road, as individuals or as a couple. I thank God we did at least have each other, even though it often felt we were not doing each other much good for quite some time. I saw a new side of my previously steady and rock-like husband, and I had to learn to relate to him in a new way as a very broken and sad man. This very broken and sad man needed to carry on with his work of leading a large and demanding parish. This was a cause of tension between us as I could see he was not really fit for the task, but for Graeme it was a way of holding on to something solid, even though it was terribly hard. For practical reasons too, as a newcomer with his feet barely under the desk, he felt that to take some extended time off at this stage may have made it too difficult to ever come back, and he wasn't sure if this was what he really wanted. To be sure, neither of us had any idea of what we wanted. All we knew was that this was no time to make any major decisions as our minds weren't working well and we'd probably get it wrong. So for now, it was a case of plodding on as best we could and praying that those around us might understand our inevitable limitations and be patient with us while we learnt to live in our new world.

Bereaved mother – saying it how it was

I can only say I felt ripped apart by the experience of losing Jim. My world, my hopes, my expectations, even maybe my faith in God had been blown apart, and now it felt as if the pieces were lying shattered at my feet. I knew I had a good husband and wonderful children and grandchildren to pour my love on, and I counted my blessings in these respects; but the simple fact remained that Jim was gone and I didn't know what to do. I didn't know where to find comfort.

My journal, written two months after his death, perhaps says it better than I can now:

Emptiness – the vessel that held you is empty. It was so full for so long and then suddenly emptied. What do I do with all the space that is left – where Jim was? That space cannot be filled by anything or anyone else. Yes, I know love and am surrounded by love, but the space that is left empty will be empty for ever. It is my 'Jim' space. Somehow I need to refill that gap, that hole, that emptiness. It is the space that is Jim. It can't be anything else. I don't know what this means yet, but maybe one day, as time passes, I'll find out.

The loss of Jim feels like a raw wound. Just like he had a room with his name on it, so he had a room in my heart with his name on it. Now the room is empty and bare. Still his. How do I face each day like this?

Later I found this quote of Dietrich Bonhoeffer in Dave Tomlinson's very helpful book, *Running into God*:

Nothing can make up for the absence of someone we love . . . it is nonsense to say that God fills the gap; God doesn't fill it, but on the contrary, God keeps it empty and so helps us keep alive our former communion with each other, even at the cost of pain . . . the dearer and richer the memories, the more difficult the separation. But gratitude changes the pangs of memory into tranquil joy.[3]

This gave validity to my own feelings. The feeling of emptiness was understood and recognised by others. I became gradually aware, as I read, reflected, walked and prayed or just sat, that I didn't need to be anything other than what I was at that time – a terrible mess – because God knew all about it and was with me in all the pain and squalor of the situation. I chose to believe and hang on to this despite the fact that that was not how it felt. Just yet, I was unable to understand about the promised 'tranquil joy', and wasn't even sure if that was where I wanted to get to, as always in the earlier months of bereavement I had a nagging feeling that if I ever 'got over it', maybe it meant I didn't love Jim enough.

At this time I felt I was in a wilderness: a desert, rocky, lonely place. The tender new shoots I had tried to nurture in our new home and community felt as if they had been cruelly ploughed up and left languishing on the thin soil of my life. My days were almost entirely unstructured as I had not managed to find employment, and had recently enrolled on a foundational counselling course in the hope that it would provide me with a new direction for my life. Consequently, I found I had a great deal of spare time on my hands. I can see now that in some ways this was a blessing for me, but in other ways it was very hard. When I needed motivation to get up in the morning there was no motivation because there was often nothing in my diary for me to do. It was only a short step to feeling an utter sense of failure in every area of my life, from my role as a mother to being a person with the value and dignity of a 'real job'. I wrote then of 'a sense of disconnectedness – lack of interest, enthusiasm, energy. Like loose strings blowing in the wind, there is no music – that is what my life feels like, unconnected, blowing in the wind.'

Sometimes it is difficult to discern when the deep pain of bereavement has turned into depression. It seems to me that there is a very thin line between the two. Often I would ask myself whether this was depression and did I need extra help, and though I still don't truly know the answer to that question, I observed that I was still able to function in important ways. I enjoyed my food, my weight was stable, I got some sleep, albeit broken, and I did get up each morning and do whatever tasks there were to do, despite the temptation to hide under the duvet. So I would usually conclude that my raging emotions were just something I had to deal with. Ironically, one of the requirements of my new course was that I should attend counselling sessions on my own behalf, to discuss anything that the course material unearthed in me. This was remarkably timely as I was able to use that time to unload my grief on my long-suffering counsellor, and this was of inestimable support to me.

Every day was much like the one before, except for Sundays – and they were even worse. Then I had a choice of being on my own, which didn't feel very positive, or of going along to church. I nearly always chose to go to church; this after all was the pattern of my life as a Christian and over many years of marriage to a church minister. Over this time though it became a place where I was subject to many conflicting and often uncomfortable emotions. I couldn't understand why it felt so hard. It should have been a safe place and there were many very warm and kind people there to whom I owe a debt of gratitude for their patience over a long time. Eventually, I discovered the idea of emotional dissonance, through the writing of Ron Dunn, an American pastor who lost his own son some years ago.[4] He helped me understand that what I was experiencing when walking into church was a kind of discord between what the socially constructed and well-behaved part of me felt I should be like – smiling, gracious, concerned for others and ready to join in with praise and worship to God – and what I really felt like: desperate, dark, angry with God and life. Emotionally, walking into church on my own felt like the equivalent of scratching your fingers down an old blackboard, it was almost physically painful.

I know, in reality, I didn't have to 'be' anything at all at that time; I only needed to be what I was – a profoundly hurting person crying out to God from the depths of my soul; but it was just so hard. How could the 'vicar's wife' (a label that I challenge, incidentally, with all the outdated assumptions that go with it!) be a sobbing, heaving ball of distress at the back of church while the vicar did his best to negotiate his way through a church service? I felt angry with God, angry with people for looking happy, angry with myself and life. Above all I felt angry with Graeme, who was doing his job upfront but was not, as far as I was concerned, doing what I needed – being beside me in an extremely isolated and painful place. In fact, we were both doing our wobbly best to simply survive in a situation we both found almost intolerable. Perhaps we went about it the wrong way, but we did the best we could. They were grim times indeed.

Each new dawning day was accompanied by a sinking stomach as I wondered how I would get through it, but I came to realise with help from my counsellor, that these desolate, blank days were very important to me as part of the process of beginning to remake meaning and connection in my life. Long and lonely as many days were for me then, they also gave me the time I needed to read, write and reflect on our loss, which was an important part of my survival. So in some sense these days were a gift to me, and now I am grateful that I had a natural pause in my life which gave me all the space and more that I needed to ponder what losing Jim meant to me.

Gradually, I began to understand that the best way of surviving was by engaging with the pain, not by trying to deny it; something I would have found impossible anyway. Now I began to learn that whatever messages I might be receiving from our busy culture which allows too little time for the messy business of grief, and from my own internal critic, that voice inside which said I should be doing better, there was a different way. There was no anaesthetic that could deal with this pain, and trying to be brave wouldn't get me far. The most healing route, I concluded, was to stick with it for as long as it took, to explore it, read about it, reflect on it and believe that though it was horrible, ultimately the loss of Jim and all that pain would not be wasted.

I still had to 'do it' though, and it was tough facing up to the questions and the feelings which were all part of the process. In the words of Richard Rohr, another writer who helped me reorientate my life over this time, I needed to 'stay with the pain of life, without answers, without conclusions and sometimes without meaning'; not an easy task and one for which I needed every last bit of my courage and determination.[5]

The process of bereavement has been much researched and analysed, and various models have been put forward by experts to help us understand it. I am not an expert, just an ordinary mum trying to understand how to live in the light of my changed world. As I have read about these models, it seems to me they all contain some degree of truth. Each one adds something helpful to the overall picture of what grief involves, if applied carefully and sensitively. One such model was defined by William Worden as the 'four tasks of grieving'.[6] Very briefly, the tasks are to accept the reality of the loss, to work through the pain of grief, to adjust to an environment in which the deceased is missing and to relocate the deceased and move on with your life. (The latter task written in a few words like this sounds callous, but further reading reveals the deeper meaning.) This was helpful to me because I was able now to grasp that what I was doing was 'work' – and it was hard. It helped me understand that while I seemed to be rather idle, actually there was a lot going on for me, and these were not wasted days.

Why?

Losing Jim challenged my long-held and sometimes painfully worked out belief in a personal, loving God. This was despite the fact that I had never been in tune with the kind of Christianity that is too glib and easy, somehow believing that God would protect from all ills and if he didn't then either something was wrong with your faith or there was some hidden sin in your life. So I never once believed I had the keys to ensuring happy endings to life's problems. There are many reasons for this, the first of which is that following Jesus never has been a guarantee of a smooth passage through life. If we needed any proof of that we only have to read about the persecution endured by the earliest disciples.

Beyond this obvious point I have to admit to being a bit too much like Eeyore, the downhearted donkey in the Winnie the Pooh stories. You can't help feeling sorry for him, with his tendency to believe that things will always go wrong. There is a degree of Eeyoreishness in me, which I am well aware of and on which I have to work on a regular basis. However, a much more significant reason lies, I believe, in witnessing the terrible decline of my sweet mother over many years, through an unusual form of dementia. I experienced utter helplessness and felt very inadequate. I could do nothing to help her and it broke my heart. Even my prayers were unable to change the situation one way or the other, it seemed. Her illness, spread over a long period of time from my early teens to my thirties, helped to shape me into the person I became, both positively and negatively. I have also been close to many other people's suffering through my career as a nurse, and later through involvement in pastoral work in the parish. Bad things do happen to good people – all the time. The question shouts out, as it always has, 'Where is God in all this?'

It is tempting and natural when disaster knocks on your door to wonder if God actually cares, or has the power to change things anyway. Indeed, in one well-known and much-quoted book on suffering, *When Bad Things Happen to Good People*, the author argues that God does care greatly but doesn't have the supernatural power to change certain situations. Rabbi Kushner, who endured the long and ultimately fatal illness of his son Aaron, concludes that God is loving but limited and can't alter outcomes as we may wish but instead changes us. Then we can more easily bear our pain, whatever it may be, by finding within ourselves courage, by reminding us that there are many who are supporting us and that there is still much to be grateful for. The book is gentle, encouraging and compassionate, but for me ultimately rather sad.[7]

I believe faith in Jesus takes us beyond this conclusion, though it doesn't provide us with easy answers or take away the pain. Instead we have to grapple with a God who we believe could change things but, for reasons we don't understand, often chooses not to. Through engaging with my own deep pain and the fundamental questioning of many of my assumptions, I found eventually that ideas I always believed about God have become more deeply rooted in my understanding of who God is and how he relates to me or any of us. I believe we see the reaction of God to suffering in the person of Jesus. Jesus reacts with great compassion to the sadness and pain he witnessed in his time on earth, and I believe that now he is alongside us, weeping with us. I believe he wept when Jim died and that he has wept with us in our grief. One book, *Lament for a Son*, has helped me greatly. It became a constant companion for a while when I discovered it a few months after losing Jim.[8] The author writes so heartrendingly and honestly about his grief for his son, who died in a mountaineering accident, and asks so many questions of God before finally concluding beautifully that God weeps too and that the unanswerable questions will just have to wait.

I have had to accept that there is no answer to 'Why?' that satisfies. The only response, and it is not easy, is, 'Trust anyway'. The prophet Habakkuk, who was alive in the seventh century before Christ, wrestled with the same age-old question, wondering why so many bad things were happening all around him and why God wasn't doing anything. He ends with a great acclamation of trust:

> Though the fig tree doesn't blossom
> and no fruit is on the vines;
> Though the produce of the olive fails
> and the fields yield no food . . .
> Yet I will rejoice in the Lord;
> I will exult in the God of my salvation.
> God, the Lord, is my strength.[9]

On the face of it this may sound simple, but it is far from simplistic, as we who call ourselves followers of God have to grapple with trust in all the situations of our lives. It means 'trusting a God who lets babies die and good people suffer'.[10] It means being willing to live in a place of 'not knowing', but fixing our eyes on Jesus and walking anyway.

The passing of time

One of the ideas commonly found in popular culture is that eventually time will heal our wounds and that we will 'get over it'. I don't believe it is as simple as this, and when I was newly bereaved of Jim I found the suggestion of such ideas very upsetting. Reflecting on the idea of time as a healer I wrote a few lines called 'Five months after':

> Never say to me that time heals . . .
> It is a cruel lie.
> Time can't heal broken things
> Like lives and hearts
> And hopes and dreams.
> Time can't heal grief.
> What is time anyway?

Five months . . . is that a long time?
How long is a piece of string?
How long is five months?
It measures nothing,
It means nothing . . .
Nothing to me.
Nothing that matters
Compared to a mother's love,
Poured out.

An anniversary of a loss is always painful. The seventh day of every month was hard at first, and then inevitably we came to half a year between us and Jim. On 7th May I went down to our local beach and sat in the spring sunshine watching the incoming tide slowly encroach on me until it was silently lapping round my feet. I wrote then that six months was a milestone we didn't want to pass. 'Not a travelling towards but a travelling away from – a leaving, a distancing in time and space, and it really hurts.' I suppose, though we count our days and calculate distances for our convenience, time and space are not simply linear, and while in human terms I felt that physically I was going further away from Jim, this was untrue in the spiritual dimension. Perhaps he was closer to me now than he was in Hong Kong, because I was learning to 'carry him in my heart'. I no longer had to worry about motherly fears of being 'overprotective' or 'tying him to my apron strings' and I could relate to him in a new way.

The concept of carrying a person in your heart sounds strange, I know, and a friend recently asked me what I meant. It was a good question and perhaps best answered in the words of a poem I wrote around this time called 'Safely carried':

I carry you in my heart
Like a photo in a wallet.
You are imprinted there – not in chemicals that will fade
But in love, indelible and non-removable,
I can't lose you or drop you or mislay you –
You are safely held for ever.

It was about this time that we attended a day arranged for
bereaved parents, as part of Care for the Family's Bereaved Parent's Support.[11] We went along with a great deal of trepidation,
not knowing what to expect, but found it to be very helpful.
Until then we had felt so horribly alone with our grief, despite
the support and love we had been given. It was not that we
doubted that many cared, and often that was shown in practical
ways, but the grief felt like a straightjacket bolted together with
painful emotions and we didn't know how to break out of it. On
whom could we risk spilling such painful feelings? It just seemed
too awful to dump it on anyone as it really was – too heavy and
too much to ask. Through the bereavement day we began to
find that we were not alone. Here we met with others who had
walked a similar road either some years before us, or even more
recently than us. We were at last able to listen to speakers who
had survived and were surviving child loss, to talk with other
parents, and recognise that not only were we not mad in having
extreme feelings, we were not even unusual. It was the beginning of breaking through some of the isolation that is a part of
grief, and maybe especially the grief of child loss, which is not
a particularly common occurrence in our Western culture and
a reversal of our expectations of how life works, which leaves
many around us uncertain how to respond.

We were told then what we had already understood, that this
grief would be part of our lives for ever. While we could not put
the grief down, we could develop the muscles to carry it more

comfortably, just as you gradually develop muscles to help you with any new task that at first seems too hard for you.

Three months before that important day I had written in my journal:

> Grief is like a heavy burden strapped to your back – although an invisible one to other people. You can't put it down. You are forced to carry it everywhere with you; it never leaves you for a moment. My prayer is that as I carry this burden I may get stronger to bear it better . . . less fatigued by it and more sure-footed again. I hope that as I 'carry' Jim, my beloved son, the joy and love will balance the weight of grief and help me to walk more truly.

But these were very early days, and at that time such words were just musings, untested by experience. It was helpful, a few months later, to hear similar ideas expressed, and I began to appreciate more deeply that there were other people out there who were able to support me as I walked this desolate, heavy-burdened path; who could provide me with enough light to move forward, small step by small step.

Guidance comes in many ways, sought and unsought. At about this time I also discovered the poems of Mary Oliver, an American author who delights in the natural world around her. She had reflected on her own grief using her rich poetic skills and once again I realised how much I could learn from others who were willing to share their insights gained through bitter experience. One poem, 'Heavy', beautifully describes how we, in time, can learn to bear the awful unlooked-for weight of grief and also acknowledges that there is part of us that would choose not to put it down, even if we could.[12]

As the shock of immediate loss passed, I began to realise that I had some choices in how I responded to losing Jim. I could choose to become bitter and somehow smaller, or I could choose to grow through the painful process. I knew innately this was what I wanted. Jim had already lost his life and I was determined that I would not lose mine as well, by shrinking and becoming embittered. I felt that that would dishonour Jim's memory, and I did not want that to happen. Reflecting on the bereavement day I wrote,

> The way I rebuild my life will be my tribute to Jim. My deep desire is to find meaning in all of this for my life. I have choice – I can choose to let my loss obliterate my life or I can choose to move forward. I choose LIFE, Jim – because in my life will be your life continuing. I am proud of you.

Writing positively like this was one thing, of course, and doing it in real life quite another. Still, that was my decision and I was determined then to see it through, and four years later, I still am.

1 Early days, 1989. Jim, Chloe, Hannah and Tom

2 Jim's first day at school, 1990

3 Relaxing at home, 2003

4 Walking the dog, 2004

5   The day before leaving for Hong Kong, 2004

6   Jim with his Grandpa on his 80th birthday, 2006

7   Hannah, Tom, Jim and Chloe, 2006

8   Jim and Tom playing football with other boys,
St Stephen's Society, Hong Kong

CHAPTER 7

Bereavement by Addiction

However it happens, bereavement hurts like hell, and if hell is separation from our living, loving God, then maybe our human losses do in some way mirror that ultimate separation, as we suffer the pain of being cut off from those we love. The world becomes a dark and fearful place for a time. Each day becomes a personal hell through which we have to negotiate our way and discover for ourselves whether we can find a way out.

The pain can become even more unbearable when the cause of death is not one that is socially easy to accept. Many deaths may come into such a category: suicide, driving when drunk, sexual games that go wrong, for example, and the one that concerns me most here, death by an overdose of illegal drugs. There may be several reasons for this, but the one I want to consider is that the bereaved may fear a negative reaction from other people which may lead to feelings of shame, stigmatisation and consequent isolation.

For a long time after Jim died I struggled with terrible feelings. I was unable to rid myself of the fear that Jim's death would be perceived as not particularly important and not particularly sad, as he was 'only a drug addict' and 'taking drugs was his choice'. The weight I felt as a result, the great loneliness of my situation, bore down on me heavily.

I attended a training event nearly two years after Jim died, run by the NHS for people who worked with homeless people, and the participants were invited to call out the words commonly associated with drug users. They quickly responded with names like smack heads, scumbags, dope heads, junkies and thieves. I felt such pain. To me, Jim was none of these things, he was just my boy who was tragically lost and I loved him so much. Who could really understand how I felt? I also wondered if others judged me as a parent for the manner of my son's death. Nearly every day it seemed I would turn on the radio and there would be another story of a drug abuser who had committed a terrible crime, or an item on the cost of drug abuse to society. It seemed to fill the airwaves. I read one article in *The Guardian* about ways in which drug users might be kept safer that began with the words, 'We may not like drug users but . . .'[1] I longed to respond to such lazy, unthinking words by shouting, 'Hey – that's my son you're talking about, a human being with a life story and feelings, just like you.'

In recent years we have heard of so many tragic deaths of young men and women in the wars in Iraq, Afghanistan and elsewhere. Each time I hear of another soldier who falls in battle my heart cracks for the family left bereaved. However, it really hurt me to hear one bereaved parent say in an interview that at least his son had 'died a hero, not like a drug addict'. I understand and respect why that man felt proud of his son, but the words cut deeply, as I knew they would make an impact on all who heard them and drive home a little deeper the message that drug users are not as worthy of our sympathy as other people who die in tragic circumstances.

I felt that I was struggling with two related but different issues. The first was bereavement and the second was the manner of the bereavement. I looked for help in many places but found little specialist information that related to my feelings as the mother of a young person who died of drug use. Yet it was hardly as if I was the first; sadly, many young men and women die in such a way. There were others out there, but I didn't know how to contact them and find the support that I needed. There seemed to be some help offered to those caught in addiction, and even to families living with the problem, but after death it felt like there was nothing. So I continued to flounder in my sense of aloneness, loving Jim, proud of who he was and what he achieved in his life, but also anxious that no one outside the family really cared that much because he was 'just a druggie'. This felt like my personal cross to bear, and every day I had to take it up and carry on and function in a world where I didn't know if anyone really understood just how proud I was of Jim and just how much it hurt.

Sadly, I think it likely that my feelings were exacerbated by the facts of our life. We were Christian people and had tried to follow Jesus, as best we could, all our married lives. In addition, Graeme was a Christian leader, week by week preaching a gospel of hope and love, and could be thought of as in some ways carrying a responsibility, not to be perfect, but to model a Christian quality of life. If we couldn't look after and protect our own children, what sort of role models were we? It was hard for me to walk into the heart of our Christian community week after week carrying this enormous weight, the fear of being judged and found wanting as a parent, and I feel the irony of that. Surely among a community of people who were seeking to follow Jesus, our radical God who always looked out for the people that the other religious leaders preferred to ignore, I should have felt certain of love and acceptance, but instead I felt a deep sense of shame and loneliness. I want to emphasize that neither in nor out of the church community did anyone say anything to me that suggested we were anything less than accepted for who we were; rather, this was how I felt, it was the pain I carried within myself. I express it now only in the hope that others who find themselves in a similar situation may feel more able to do something about that pain than I was, or at least know that they are not alone in feeling that way.

For six months after Jim died, we didn't tell anyone what had caused his death, for one simple reason: we didn't really know ourselves. We certainly strongly suspected that drugs had killed him, but we didn't conclusively know this until after the inquest. Until then we were officially 'not sure'. It says a lot about how we felt about the way he had died, that we hoped, until the last moment, another cause might be found – perhaps after all he had died of a brain haemorrhage or an unsuspected heart defect. Had that turned out to be the case, we could still salvage his reputation and ours as well.

In writing in this way I am saying a lot about myself that I don't like very much. It reveals to me that I too had my prejudices about shameful and not shameful causes of death. If Jim had to die at all, then I would have preferred he had died of something 'respectable', something that my friends could relate to more easily, something that was 'not his fault'. That might sound crazy, for after all, what could be worse than Jim dying? If I am honest, though, that is how it was; I would have preferred not to have to deal with the whole drug issue if it could have been avoided. But here we were, it was unavoidable, and we now had to learn to live openly with the fact that our son had died of a heroin overdose.

As I have been on this very steep course of learning, I have discovered many things. One of the most important of these was that in some respects we might be considered fortunate. Those who see their beloved family members get lost deep in drug and alcohol addiction often talk of being bereaved twice. They may experience the pain of seeing their loved one change character as the drug gets hold of them. The user may become deceitful, manipulative and hurtful to those he or she loves most, as they become lost to the powerful grip of the substance. The drug becomes the master, and other normal relationships sink to secondary importance. Many families will talk of the terrible shame experienced as their loved one descends further and further into the grip of addiction.[2] Many will live for years with that shame and the fear of what may happen next. Then, sadly, if the worst comes to the worst, they may need to face a second bereavement when their loved one dies. For us it was a different story – we didn't even know that Jim was involved with dangerous drugs until he died, and so we were able to retain our image of the young man we knew and loved. Others' stories may go on for years, until they even have trouble remembering what their son or daughter was like before drugs took charge. I don't know how Jim's story might have developed had he lived. I like to think that together we might have been able to beat the addiction and he might have had a story of overcoming, as so many others do; but that wasn't to be, and really I don't know. Which of us are the better off – those who live with a flicker of hope for years, or those whose hope of recovery is extinguished by death at an early stage? That is another question with no easy answer.

Of coroners' courts and newspaper people

Everyone loves a good story, and never more so than if a vicar or someone known in the community is involved. To our horror, within one or two days of Jim's death we found the story being written about in the local and national papers. We were so used to reading or hearing of other people's tragedies, and it came as a terrible shock to suddenly find we were the ones being written about. How, exactly, do the media find out? We felt very vulnerable when we discovered that reporters had been snooping round our home, looking through the windows and hoping to get some 'good copy' at our Jim's expense. It was genuinely hard to understand why anyone else should have any interest in our personal disaster. Thankfully we were away at the time and we are grateful to our friends who dealt with the press for us.

Six months after his death, we had to attend the coroner's

inquest. We knew it was here that the full story would come out and we were still anxious to save Jim's reputation as far as possible. We knew that reporters would be present and keen to present a good story to their editors. We also knew it wasn't personal of course; they just had their job to do, like it or not.

One of the hard things about any death is the need to deal with aspects of life we know little about. Not many of us are experts at arranging funerals, not many of us know exactly by when you should have registered a death. This is true in any bereavement. In a case where death is unexpected and the definite cause is unknown, it all becomes even more complicated. Now you find yourselves involved with the police and the coroner's court, tied up with processes about which you probably know nothing and which can seem very confusing, and all this at a time when you are barely functioning anyway. For us, there were further complications since Jim had died overseas, and we had to deal with a different system altogether. We never knew if we got as much information as we would have, had he died in England, but we had to live with the way things were.

Back in England, meanwhile, our experience was that the coroner's office, whose staff are sadly used to family tragedies, looked after us very well and were happy to explain the process and answer any questions we had. We were dreading the day of the inquest itself, and there certainly is not much good to be said for hanging around in an impersonal coroner's court waiting-room. Once again, we were in a surreal world where it was hard to believe this was happening to us, but in the event we felt we were treated very respectfully, and we remain grateful for this. Although for the coroner it was a fairly routine case, we felt he was kind and considerate and did his best in a formal, legal setting to offer us his compassion. We had prepared for the press in advance by writing out a press release, as we had been advised to do by a friend who knew more about the media than us. When the reporters asked us questions we offered them the release which they took happily enough. There was no guarantee they would refer to it in any subsequent report but, in the end, they used it almost word for word. Perhaps we saved them a job!

It was at this point we faced up to sharing openly the cause of Jim's death. We knew that the result of the inquest would be published in papers both in the east and west of Cheshire and many who knew us would read it. Now there was no hiding, so we decided to stick our chins out and go for it. We wrote an article to be given out in the churches where we had lived and worked, thinking that if there was going to be any gossip or shock, it was best to put the truth as we understood it into people's hands, so at least the facts would be correct. I wrote in my journal later,

> Everybody knows now; no more secrets. A bit like lancing a boil, but even though the secret is out, there is no healing. The sadness just pours and pours. I feel naked, vulnerable and exposed and yet certain this was the best thing to do. Paradoxically, it is the last thing we want to do, but feel we have little or no choice in the matter. Our main concern is that Jim is honoured and not judged.

My defensiveness is clear to myself, as I read this now. It illustrates rather well the shame that we felt, I suppose. Others who know us may feel shocked and even hurt to know we felt so anxious about being judged. I think it actually says more about us, or perhaps me, and our sense of shame than about other people. I was judging myself and expecting to be judged. I ask myself now how would I have responded if it had been the son or daughter of one of my friends; would I have judged them or felt they had failed? I think I would have had only sympathy for them, so I wonder why I was afraid they might be harsher to me. So often we are our own harshest critics. It seems strange to say that if only Jim hadn't died of such a cause, it would have all been a bit easier to cope with, but I am afraid it is true anyway.

Where was God in all this?

I know now that God was much more in it than I was. Whereas I recoiled from becoming part of the world of drugs with all my prejudices and preconceptions, God was right there, in the mess, and always has been. I see Jesus mixing with the down and outs, not afraid to get his hands dirty, partying with the marginalised and despised. God does not recoil from addicts and alcoholics, any more than he recoils from me with my self-righteous, sometimes rather priggish attitudes. In fact, I have an uncomfortable feeling he might find them rather better company; but thankfully for me, our God is loving and forgiving. God has spoken to me so loudly and clearly through my experience of losing Jim in this way. I have had to face up to parts of myself I don't like very much at all. I am grateful to Jim that, in his death, he has taught me so much. I have been to places I never thought I would go to and sat with people I never thought I would have anything in common with; but as we know, death is a great leveller. Perhaps one of my most cherished memories is of sharing Jim's story in a drug rehabilitation centre in England and one of the men there commenting that until then he had thought of himself as scum, but if it could happen to 'people like us too' (that's to say, from his perspective, clean-living educated folk) then maybe he was all right too. I felt a big 'Amen' rising in my chest then. 'No, you are not scum, nor was Jim and nor are we. We are just poor wounded men and women trying to live in a broken and confusing world as best as we can and we all mess up in one way or another. We're in this together.'

Through Jim's death, God took me to a liminal place, a thin threshold where I was able to see differently for a while. It was a place of great pain and deeper learning than I had known before. My prayer now is that lessons learnt then will fully embed and may continue to bear fruit in my life in the years to come. In that way, Jim's life will also go on.

'He died of shame'

I have spoken about the shame that I felt when Jim died and how we had to face up to what we feared other people might think of him, or us. But what about Jim himself, I wonder – what part did shame play in his death? One of the first things we did when we arrived in Hong Kong after he died was to spend time with Jackie Pullinger, who had known Jim as well as anyone in the last years of his life. Jackie told us that in her opinion he had died of shame. What did she mean by this, exactly? It seems to us that Jim had set high standards for himself which he felt unable to attain. He longed to overcome his problems and to achieve something with his life. He longed to be free from the power of drugs, and yet there seemed to be a draw that was stronger than he was. After his death we were given a letter written by him to some friends that graphically describes the battle he was in. He wrote about standing at a bus stop in Shatin knowing he could choose one bus that would take him to a dealer or he could choose the other that would take him home to St Stephen's and safety. On that occasion he made the right choice. We know that finally when he was discovered with heroin in his possession he was deeply ashamed, and that showed itself in confusion and anger. The shame of discovery, of it becoming public knowledge that he wasn't winning the battle, overcame him and resulted in him trying to hide from the very people who could help him. Sadly he chose to look for help from a friend of his who was as vulnerable as he was, and in the end Jim's choices resulted in his death.

As Jim's parents we have had to ask ourselves whether we were responsible for imposing standards that were too high for him to attain. Was his sense of shame a result of our efforts to instil a certain value system in our children? Maybe he simply felt he couldn't live up to our expectations. I'm not going to try and answer these questions, as I realise nobody can ever really know the truth about what happens in the heart of another person. This is one of those areas I have to leave unanswered. All I know is we did our best to love him from the beginning to the end, and we still love him. We have had to come to terms with the drug issue in death, and I am sure we would have come to terms with it in life, had we been given that choice. I have since talked to many parents who are struggling with difficult issues in their family life and who wonder if they are to blame. My response is: if you can look at yourself in a mirror and say honestly, 'I did my best', then how can you blame yourself when things go wrong? There are no perfect parents; we all make mistakes and get things wrong and the most powerful and healing thing we can do is to acknowledge this and to say sorry.

Breaking the isolation

For two long years Graeme and I battled on. There were some good times and many things to enjoy in life, but underlying even the good days was a pervading sense of weariness and distress. At the second anniversary of Jim's death I found myself feeling just as bad as I had at the first. In fact in some ways I felt worse, as I really felt I should be doing a lot better by now. I had reached a point where I seriously wondered if I might be near some kind of breakdown and I hardly knew where to turn for help. I tried ringing a telephone support line for bereaved parents, and though the listener was kind, it was clear that he wasn't really sure how to respond to this form of bereavement – I'm not knocking that man or the service offered, but I don't think the area had been covered in the volunteer training. Eventually and possibly just in time to save me sinking even lower, a friend put a book into my hands and said I might find it helpful. The book, *Mum, Can You Lend Me Twenty Quid?*, was written by a woman who had lost her own son after a long struggle with heroin.[3] As a result of that book and the many contacts it gave the author, she and others had recently established a new charity called DrugFam, based in High Wycombe in Buckinghamshire, with the expressed aim of helping families coping with addiction issues, before or after bereavement.[4] At last we were able to speak to people like us, people who knew what this bereavement felt like, others who understood the sense of shame, stigma and isolation that accompanied it. At last we were not alone. Less than two weeks after first hearing of DrugFam, we were able to attend their first annual 'Bereaved by Addiction' conference, in November 2009. It was very tough, and even there we felt vulnerable, but that was OK; I wasn't the only one who spent much of the day in tears. It is hard to tell of the strength that is gained by knowing you are no longer alone. The conference sessions were given by a combination of ordinary parents like us and experts working in the field, who bowled us over with the obvious love and compassion that they felt for both the addicts and their families. Although in many ways the day was emotionally wearing, we headed off up the motorway at the end of it, knowing that others were struggling with many of the same issues as us. We now felt less stigmatized and isolated.

Discovering DrugFam and the specific support offered there marked a significant point in both our journeys of recovery. The contacts and friendships begun there led us to attending other relevant training events in the coming year, until in November 2010 we returned to the conference for a second time. This time we were invited to participate as speakers to share some of our experiences and what we felt had both helped and hindered us in our bereavement. That I had travelled from being in a place of such lostness and despair in November 2009 to being able to share with others some of the insights I had gained, just one year later, is a powerful sign of the therapeutic benefit of having companionship and community, even if the community in question is wide flung. Before discovering DrugFam, I had had my books, my journal, my friends, my solitude and my faith that God was somehow with us in all the mess, but I had still felt essentially alone. Now I knew I wasn't, and with that knowledge I felt less ashamed, less stigmatized and, eventually, able to hold my head higher.

Stories of victory or stories of failure?

I have talked about some of the particular issues faced when someone you love dies in a 'shameful' way. In learning to live with our situation, I have had to face up to many of my own demons around failure, shame and anxiety about how others may perceive us, especially with the added dimension of Graeme's role as a leader in the church. There was one other factor too, which probably is only relevant to those of us who are part of faith communities, and believe in a God who heals us and restores us. It isn't easy to be a Christian in a sceptical and hurting world, and consequently we love to be encouraged by stories of victory and triumph over adversity. Those with amazing stories to tell are very popular on the speaking circuits for obvious reasons, as we are all eager to find encouragement to help us live our faith more positively. I think there may be a downside to this, however, which is to ignore how God is with us in all the situations of our lives, both when we enjoy success and when we encounter failure. There are lessons for faith in both success and failure, but maybe we learn the richer lessons when life is hard. Are we as ready to learn the lessons of failure as we are to embrace the successes of life? Dave Bookless, who headed up the UK work of an environmental organisation called A Rocha, has encountered great suffering in his family life. He came and spoke in our church and told how, when he and his wife went on to experience dramatic healing, they were greatly in demand by churches to tell their story, but when they had been living through years of sadness and sorrow there was considerably less interest in them. Dave comments, 'In the end we only accepted invitations from churches where we were free to talk not only about how God works through healing, but about all that God can do through pain and suffering as well.'[5] It is true that pain and sadness don't often make great stories, but we need to be aware that God is just as much at work in those times where everything goes pear-shaped, as when everything goes well. If we don't look for the lessons in all situations we risk missing out a lot of what God wants to teach us.

CHAPTER 8

Walking with a Limp

Whatever hits us in life, however terrible, there are always choices to be made which revolve around how we react to the events which have had such an impact on us. In the immediate days, weeks and months after a severe trauma we may not be able to think clearly about 'What now?', but that time will surely come as other parts of our lives keep inexorably moving forward, even though we may wish they would give us a break for a while. It is a cliché to say that 'life goes on', but like most clichés it is basically true.

We faced our next family crisis, even before we had had Jim's funeral, as we returned from Hong Kong to find my father seriously ill in hospital. It seemed quite likely that we might have been arranging two funerals at once at one stage. He recovered partially, however, and instead I became the carer of a very ill and vulnerable parent who was also facing up to bereavement in many ways – loss of his health and independence as well as the loss of his grandson. For me, it felt there was just too much to cope with, and there were many times when I thought I just wasn't going to make it, physically, emotionally or spiritually. My father lived sixteen months beyond Jim in the end and without doubt those sixteen months were terribly hard for both of us. In the months after Jim died, we also did what we could for Hannah and her family while she suffered potentially serious pregnancy complications, and helped Tom prepare for his wedding. He married Ele nine months after losing his brother, and Hannah's healthy baby Ted was born a month after this. During this same period we walked with a close friend and colleague while she suffered the terminal stages of cancer, and she finally died four weeks after my father. No wonder, as I look back, I felt on the edge.

The walking wounded

It was during these demanding months that I coined the phrase 'walking with a limp' to describe for myself how I thought the rest of my life would work out. As far as I was concerned, I was going to be permanently marked by losing Jim and would bear the wound of deep grief in my soul for ever. The question I asked myself was, did this have to be seen as a negative response to the loss, or were there ways in which it could be seen as positive? To me, the limp was a metaphor, expressing my deep woundedness, whether or not that wound was obvious on the outside or only apparent to God and myself. As I began to explore this, I realised I was hardly the first person to think in such terms.[1] Many other people had been there before me and had showed me it was possible to survive terrible tragedies and to carry the wounds with grace. This is something I have learnt from walking through my own personal furnace – when you go through deep trauma of any kind, it is natural for a while to feel as if you are the only one who has been through such pain and no one else can ever understand. After a while you realise that this is not the case and, in fact, there are many who have gone before you and can accompany you on your awful journey.

When the wounds were very fresh and exceedingly painful, however, like any animal in distress I found I wanted to curl up and hide in an attempt to shield myself from more hurt. The truth was that no amount of hiding away could shield me from the fact that Jim was gone and it was now my job, as I saw it, to discover how to live in the light of this desperately painful new reality. These were the days, weeks, months and even years when my trust in anything – God, life, myself – was put to its severest test.

I searched to find meaning and make sense of why Jim had died and why these things had happened, until eventually I understood there was no meaning to be found in his death, there was no sense; it was essentially a meaningless, pointless tragedy, like many other tragedies that happen day in, day out. Having accepted that, I was able to realise that it was actually my task to work out what it meant for me in my life. The meaning was not to be found in Jim's death, but in my response to his death.[2] How would I choose to live my life now? Could I learn from this horrible situation and, somehow taking Jim with me, grow as a person? Could I carry my wound in such a way that instead of being limited by it, I could become stronger? Here again is paradox. Can a wound make you stronger? Shouldn't the Christian way be to seek healing and to believe that in Christ we can be made whole again? Maybe the question should be, 'What is wholeness?' Does it mean perfection, or is it, in this context, embracing the whole of who we are, including our broken wounded bits, and offering it all to God? It seemed that for me this way offered most hope of healing, as I would know that the person I was becoming was a result of the terrible wound of losing Jim. I wanted this to be the 'new me' that would walk into the world, wounded most definitely, but still walking and trusting that God was with me.

I like the parable, found in Henri Nouwen's classic book, *The Wounded Healer*, of the wounded messiah who, covered in bandages, sits among the poor, tending his own wounds just one at a time.[3] He knows that if he waits passively until he is healed he will wait for ever and never be ready for others, but he also knows that if he spends too much time focusing on how to heal his own wounds, he'll never have time or energy to help others. For me, the meaning is that the choice is mine – I can allow the pain of my losses and wounds to become the focus of my life or I can allow them, in time and with the help of God, to begin to transform my understanding and to assist me in responding to my own and others' needs. This is an ongoing process for me, and I am unsure what it all means as yet, but nevertheless, I am determined.

The value of lament

It took a long time for me to even get a handle on my thoughts and feelings, and it was necessary to allow space for the terrible untidiness of grief, which expressed itself in all sorts of chaotic and confusing ways. In the long and winding way through the labyrinth of grief I had to resist the temptation to whitewash the pain or to pretend to be other than I was, though sometimes it was so much easier to say I was fine, when really I was not fine at all. Over the process I have learnt more about one powerful tool, lament, through which we can express our deepest emotions. Lament can be defined as an outpouring of deep grief and sadness, and perhaps it is not a concept that sits comfortably with some of us. Many, including me, have grown up with the idea that we should be brave and do our best not to show our feelings, as if that is somehow letting the side down. One experienced hospice chaplain comments that he has observed that frequently and ironically Christians suffer as much or even worse in bereavement than people of no particular faith. In his opinion this may be because they feel a social pressure to be 'good witnesses' and not let God down by showing too much distress.[4] I believe we need to be encouraged and allowed to voice our pain, and be true to our honest feelings before God and others as part of the process of recovery. To do so is not a sign of loss of faith, but may point to a 'deepening spiritual life' and 'a vibrant faith; one that has learnt to lift everything – everything – to the Father in prayer'.[5]

One of our most powerful experiences in Hong Kong occurred when we were sitting in our little flat, above where the men in the community met to worship. We heard the men, many of them tough, hardened men who had experienced and even inflicted much suffering during their lives, quite literally pouring their hearts out in grief for their young friend, our Jim, in a mournful expression of lament we will never forget. Lament has a noble history, and in many of the psalms there are examples that we may copy, if we find that this is a form of worship we are not comfortable with. Walter Breuggeman, a respected theologian, coined the term 'Psalms of Disorientation' to describe those psalms which are primarily despairing and angry outpourings of emotion to God when the writers, as men of faith, had lost their way and their hope for a while.[6] Psalm 88 is the only psalm that has no light at all in it, no alleviation of despair and hopelessness, other than the fact that the writer is still bothering to address God at all. Such psalms contain terrible expressions of grief and anger, and by reflecting on them we know we don't have to hold back on voicing our strongest emotions to God. One author comments that honesty 'is the bass line of any relationship of quality . . . if God has disappointed us by letting life go wrong . . . it's liberating to let him know'.[7]

Honest expression of anger is a part of lament and a part of learning to walk with a limp. For me, writing thoughts and feelings down became an essential way of getting through, and some of those writings reveal deep levels of anger, confusion and pain. Not everyone likes writing and it might not be helpful for some, but what is important is to find some way of allowing the painful or angry feelings to surface rather than burying them and hoping that if they are ignored long enough they may just go away. Steve Griffiths, a church minister whose wife died at a young age of a brain tumour, wrote of the risk that we may cover up our grief and anger with the possible result that 'the inner rage will increase and potentially work itself out in unhealthier and potentially more damaging ways . . . it is easy to approach God like a hypocrite using all the right words but with a heart consumed by anger – but God is not interested in our words, he wants us to share what we really feel'.[8]

Guilt

I have a feeling that guilt is closely linked with lament and anger. Guilt frequently accompanies grief, whatever the cause of the loss and however undeserved the guilt is. Somehow, when faced with the ultimate separation, few of us are immune from feeling we could or should have done more. Perhaps that is a normal human response we simply have to come to terms with. However, it is also possible for guilt to become harmful for us, when it becomes a way of turning anger towards ourselves and we feel unable to deal with it. It may then manifest in other ways, such as depression or anxiety, or turning to unhelpful methods of coping with overwhelming feelings. Guilt can become very troublesome, as I found in the aftermath of my mother's long illness and death when somehow, quite unreasonably, I felt I should have been able to do more for her. Those bleak days taught me how debilitating such heavy guilt can be. When Jim died, I had to ask myself many difficult questions about my responsibility, and it would have been very easy for me to start blaming myself. I could have felt guilty for supporting him in going to Hong Kong, for not recognising the seriousness of his problems, for not being there for him when he became so desperate towards the end, and for not being with him when he died. For all these reasons guilt hovered around me and there were times when it threatened to descend, but thankfully this time the truth was stronger. I knew I had really loved Jim and tried to do my imperfect best. He had made his own decisions and his own mistakes, and I was not responsible for that. In time I knew that I didn't need to be guilty. The loss, the pain and the confusion was already more than enough to bear.

Sometimes, however, the feelings of guilt, anger and despair brought about by grief can be so incapacitating that an individual may need help beyond that of friends and family and their own ability to heal, and it may be wise to find extra support, whether from a GP or a bereavement counsellor or both.

Facing into the pain

I am no masochist, but for me learning to walk with a limp meant having to face the pain head on. I've never had a hip operation or any other major surgery, but I imagine it is very hard to force yourself to take those first painful steps and to do the physiotherapy exercises carefully planned for your recovery. It hurts but you know you have to do it, to gain strength and get better. For me the emotional pain was a bit like this; I had to look at it, examine it and learn to flex my wounded self again. I did this in various ways, and thankfully Graeme did it with me. In the first place, we both read a great deal about bereavement and grief and searched for what we could learn from others. Then we watched a variety of films that were just very sad, often featuring bereavement and different people's responses to it. Sometimes we would end the evening with piles of soggy hankies beside us, but that was all right, and we found that in some strange way we felt better for having given ourselves opportunities to engage with painful emotions. I can't explain this, and no doubt some psychiatrist somewhere would have a field day with us, but there it is. We balanced the misery with some lighter viewing as well, and gave ourselves quite a few laughs along the way, which I think was just as important.

After a year we began to wonder if we could face returning to Hong Kong. We knew it would be hard, but we were keen to meet with Jim's friends again, and we wanted to connect with the places that had become so special to him. So fifteen months later we went back to walk again in the busy streets that had such poignant meaning for us. God was with us in some special ways on that trip. As soon as we landed we took a taxi to the community house in Shatin where a celebration weekend was being held to mark the opening of some new buildings, providing extra accommodation, education and sports facilities. We arrived a bit late and were ushered to the front of the new sports hall where a time of worship and thanksgiving was in progress. To catch the spirit of the place and to witness how much had been achieved in the short time since Jim had died was a real privilege. There was dancing, singing and praising that day as the residents and many friends of St Stephen's gathered to thank God. We joined in praising, worshipping and crying tears of joy and sadness all at the same time. During the worship Graeme had an overwhelming sense that Jim was there too, dancing with his friends. Later Jackie said how she believed that the building and all the ongoing work was redemptive and built on the work of those who had gone before, including her husband John and our Jim. She told us, 'Your Jim walked and fell, but let me tell you that he did not live a wasted life'. I understand this to mean that although there was no meaning or purpose in Jim's death, the days and years of his life were not wasted – his death remains a waste, but his time on this earth was not wasted. After the worship there was a barbecue and we were deeply moved when Jim's special friends simply came and gathered round us to be close. We were profoundly grateful and humbled by the gentle love they showed to us then. There were several young men we were praying for, Jim's closest friends there, and we were longing that they would be truly set free from their addictions; it was fantastic to see so many of them again and to hear about the progress they were making.

In the next days, we met with several people who also counted themselves among Jim's special friends – men and women older and younger than him from both East and West. What struck us deeply was the gratitude they showed us for returning to Hong Kong. This was something we never anticipated. We thought we were going for ourselves, as part of our own healing, but in fact it was also important for a number of people there who carried, unnecessarily, a burden of guilt for what had happened to Jim. It was a huge privilege to be able to talk and pray with them and to give them the freedom to put down the burden they had been carrying. One young man, whom we had never met before, was in tears after a time of worship and asked to speak to us. He told us he had been one of the lads that Jim had met in Soul Survivor back in 2000 when he was fourteen, and he had told Jim that if he came out to Hong Kong he would look after him. When Jim did finally arrive three years later, his life had moved on, he now had a job and found it hard to give Jim time around his other responsibilities. When Jim died he felt terrible remorse that had stayed with him. It was a particular joy to pray with him and to ask God to release him from any lingering feelings of guilt. We knew that nobody needed to carry guilt for what had happened to Jim. In many ways we felt that this chance to meet with individuals and pray with them to ask God to free them from any sense of guilt was one of the main reasons we had needed to go back, though it wasn't something we had foreseen.

Being among Jim's friends also gave us a chance to share memories about him and to laugh together over some of the funny ones, which was very special. Bereaved people often have a need to talk about the person they have lost, and because we now lived in a place where no one had known Jim, this had been hard for us to do. So at last we had a chance to catch up and chat to others who had also loved him.

After about ten days the time came to return to England. I had not thought about how leaving Hong Kong a second time would affect me. As the plane took off and we returned to our lives in England I revisited afresh the terrible feelings of bereavement.

It only struck me now that in some tiny irrational corner of my mind, it had been hard to accept that Jim had really died. The truth is that because he had lived away from home for two or three years before he died, his death hadn't really changed our daily routine. We hadn't set a place at the table for him for some time, for example, or had his socks in the washing basket. Maybe a part of my mind carried on with the deceit that 'Jim wasn't really dead, only in Hong Kong'. Whatever, I felt terrible when I got home, and the painful emotions were exacerbated by finding that my father had once again been taken into hospital while we were away. It felt like 'Ground Hog Day' for us as we began the routine of hospital visiting again, while nursing the wounds of refreshed loss. Ten days later my poor old Dad died and I had to come to terms with a fresh sense of grief and also guilt. I felt that, immersed in my whirlpool of sadness and sorrow, I hadn't loved and cared for him as well as I could have in his last days, and I felt terrible about this. Guilt, my old enemy, reared its ugly head again, as it did after my mother's death. It seems there are some lessons in life you have to relearn over and over again and, for me, coping with guilt is one of these.

Comfort in surprising places

Some six months before our return to Hong Kong, I had accompanied my friend and colleague, Pat, on a journey to the Democratic Republic of Congo, a beautiful country but famous for all the wrong reasons. Congo, the theatre of a terrible war between 1998 and 2003, when it is estimated up to five million died and where the repercussions still rumble on, faces many challenges which have been well documented elsewhere.[9] Pat had worked there for 25 years before returning to England and a rather quieter Upton in 2005. She was still involved with her work there but now she was seriously ill, diagnosed with terminal cancer.

In August 2008, just nine months after Jim died, a week after Tom's wedding and two weeks before Hannah's second baby was due, Pat asked me to go with her on a trip to see her many friends there one last time. I had been once before with her, in April 2007, and had found it an incredibly rich time of learning. I knew this trip would be somewhat different as both our lives had changed so much since then, but I felt that it was important to go and walk with my friend into this uncertain situation. Pat really wasn't well at all and it was quite a test of faith for both of us, but the journey will remain for ever a highlight of my life, I know. I sat among men and women, dads and mums, children, brothers, sisters, who had lived with loss, fear and humiliation in ways I could hardly imagine and yet were some of the most gracious and caring people you could ever hope to meet anywhere. It is almost impossible to describe the comfort these deeply hurting people were able to extend to me: a comfort that came from deep within their hearts, as in some of the most terrible experiences they had continued to trust in a God who cared for them. These were people with almost nothing, no access to books, classes or counsellors, who in the extremity of their situation hung on to a faith that God would not let them down and still cared for and loved them, despite the shocking suffering inflicted through the hands and weapons of brutalised soldiers and the material poverty of their lives. Men and women who had lost children came to seek me out, to sit with me and connect in our shared sorrow across the culture gap. It was truly amazing and humbling on the deepest level. I learnt so much from these dear people about living with grace in the face of appalling loss. There, lives are much more connected than ours to the four elements of fire, water, earth and sky. Perhaps people who live closer to the soil than most of us are more able to under-stand their place in the cosmos, while we, with our more artificial lifestyles, feel cut off from our roots and somehow imagine we should be able to have more control over what happens to us. It therefore comes as a greater shock when things go wrong, and we are more prone to question 'Why me?' and to feel it is unfair. Perhaps this sense that we should be able to control what happens to us is a subtle lie that pervades our culture, sold to us by our consumer society, advertising and materialism.

Pat did a great thing for me in inviting me to accompany her. It wasn't easy to leave my family just then, as Hannah was very unwell and just a week or two from giving birth to her second child. Happily, we were well supported in making the decision, not least by our friendly bishop who gave Graeme permission to take a little extra time off to support Hannah and her family, so I could be freer to go with Pat. Such generosity and under-standing was shown to us, and the payback was huge. Alongside my own personal learning I witnessed how the Congolese, who truly loved Pat, were able to openly trust her into the hands of God, even though in losing her they would lose a person that they loved as a mother.

One year later, Graeme and I returned to Congo again, this time with a different purpose. Pat died eight months after her last trip and now we wanted to return to grieve with her sur-rogate family who had loved her so well. It is always difficult when loved ones die a long way from us, and now we were able to reassure her family there that she had died peacefully with great assurance of God's love. Once again these days proved very rich for us, as we were invited into the community as part of their family, linked by our common grief, love and respect for Pat and for many of us our own, more personal experiences of child loss.

Still walking and still limping

The first eighteen months after losing Jim were an extraordi-nary time in many ways, as I grappled with losing my beloved boy and what this meant for me then and for the rest of my life. Alongside my individual struggle, we struggled as a family too, learning what his death meant for all of us. Over the same months, I had other challenges too: caring for my father, supporting my family through a wedding, illnesses and childbirth and trying my best to walk with Pat as she became more ill and debilitated by her illness. Travelling to Congo and to Hong Kong were both profound experiences and times where I was freshly aware of how God was somehow in all of this mess. But mess it was, a daily ongoing grind to keep going, through exhausting, 'treacley' times when I wondered if I would ever find my energy again. I plodded through, day in, day out, and it was very hard. I write that now, not to discourage but rather to encourage any other plodders out there who wonder if they can keep going. Somehow, when you don't think you will make it, you do – at least that is what I have found so far, and I'm still walking, although I haven't covered much distance on this particular journey, and I'm still waiting to know how it will all work out.

CHAPTER 9

Cosmos

I love books and films with stories that engage you, heart and mind, where you wonder from chapter to chapter how it is all going to turn out and how the loose ends will be tied up. A good story absorbs you, and a skilful writer makes you really care about what is going to happen, even if you know it is only fiction. Sadly, I am aware that it can never be like that in a true story such as the one told in these pages. It can only ever be the story of 'up to now' and a story which leaves us still asking the unanswerable questions: what went wrong and why did Jim die in that way?

A few months after Jim died, I had a conversation with a good friend in which I commented that maybe she should wait for five years before asking me how I was doing after losing Jim, as by then I might be able to answer more clearly. I started writing this account three years after his death, and now more than four years have passed and the learning goes on. I realise more and more how right I was in thinking about that sort of time span. Nevertheless, as I review these years, it feels necessary to try and pull a few loose ends together and to reflect on where I have got to now. I am a person who likes to make connections from one part of my life to another and to see what I can learn. I don't see one event in isolation from another and I tend to want to tie things up. Losing Jim is one event, however, that I can't tie up, so I can only look for the connections and see what I can learn.

On our second visit to Hong Kong, sixteen months after Jim died, we saw images of the beautiful Cosmos flower bloom wherever we went, as the annual Hong Kong Flower show was about to take place and Cosmos was the designated flower of the year. We had a wonderful afternoon at the flower show with Jim's friend, Angel (she's the second angel in this story – see Chapter 1!) and enjoyed the colourful displays, many of which featured Cosmos. I remembered seeing Cosmos blooming in Congo too, in utterly different circumstances, struggling through hard-baked red clay, bringing colour and beauty into small village encampments. I was never sure if it just bloomed wild or whether the people had sown it on purpose, but it looked as if it had just grown on its own and was a sign to me that there is beauty to be found everywhere, if you only stop and look. The word 'cosmos' means, among other things, harmony, order and peace, and the flower has come to symbolise these virtues and is now often associated with love. I was moved by seeing this modest but beautiful flower growing in the two places that had impacted on my soul in different ways, as I walked through so much pain and grief. I decided that my own garden would be full of these same flowers so that when I looked out, I would see them: shining in the sun, bobbing in the breeze or bowed under rain, and they would remind me of how I was connected to Hong Kong and Congo, how I had learnt so much from my links with them, painful though they were, and how, despite it all, part of me was grateful. Now spring is nearly here again and it will soon be time again to think about sowing.

So that explains why this final chapter is called 'Cosmos'. It is a sign of peace, love and harmony, of finding balance and restoration, as I continue on my shaky way through this world, bereft of Jim but grateful for all I have and refusing to give up hope that one day we will see the bigger picture.

By now, it is probably apparent that I am quite fond of metaphors as a way of trying to explain what I am feeling or trying to say. It struck me as I was thinking about it all, how often I likened my life to a journey, a struggle, a battle or a fight, and as I thought about that, I began to feel quite weary. It just made life seem very hard, so I got to wondering if there may be another metaphor, just as apt, but one that also held the possibility of rest. As I thought about this, I pondered on the creative possibilities of seeing my life as a garden instead of, or perhaps as well as, a hard journey. We are blessed in our present home in having a large, rather overgrown but somehow quite beautiful garden, and really I don't need to look farther than through my own window to see how there are many spiritual lessons just in our own patch. There I see birds feeding and getting nourishment, I see young plants growing and maturing and also the danger of them being choked by the ever-present brambles; I see the pond in the centre, built by family and friends as a gift in memory of Jim, which provides refreshment for the frogs, newts, mammals and birds and a home for many. We have a vegetable patch where we are learning how to grow a few things; and of course, when the season is right, I have my Cosmos to bring beauty, colour and remembrance. To me, when I am in a mood to see, there is a meaning to every part of the garden, and I can easily liken it to my own life. I like to think how God and I are working together on the plot, which is me, looking out for weeds, seeing some beautiful things blossom, and pruning the branches that need it to encourage further growth. The garden is also a place where I can rest and where I can observe the seasons come and go. Sometimes it is a busy, active time for growth, and other times it can seem pretty barren, as if not much is happening – rather like my life at different times.

In these days of learning to live without Jim, I think I like this image taken from nature and will hold it together with the more common one of our lives being journeys, as I find it restful and more forgiving of my frequent blunders, time wasting and weariness. When things don't work out in a garden you can always have another go, and even when really it isn't much of a garden, there are still things of beauty, like blackberries which grow from those annoying brambles.

When Jim died, I found myself in the centre of an emotional storm. I could no more control my feelings than I could stop the trees in the garden tossing around in a gale. The feelings went everywhere: anger, guilt, despair, loneliness, doubt, anxiety, all tossing about in my head, like a cage of angry monkeys, banging up against the walls of my mind and not able to find any sense of resolution. Through it all I had to do my best to support Graeme and the family (as they also did their best to support me), had to find time and energy for other local commitments, keep going with the requirements of my counselling course and, maybe hardest of all, look after my Dad in his time of great weakness and need, when I simply didn't have the energy. There were some very dark days and times when it felt utterly overwhelming. Sometimes people wonder how long it takes to 'get through grief', and my answer to that is 'as long as it takes', and even then, life won't revert to what it was; you are changed for ever. But for myself, I can clearly see now that the first two years were the worst, and I can put an exact date on the day when I began to feel that recovery might be possible. That was a heady, exhilarating feeling which I attempted to capture in some words called 'Awakening':

What is this that begins to break in?
I see light:
Like rivers of water trickling over dry sand
As the tide turns, pushing the water,
Little rivulets carving channels.
As buds swell and begin to unfurl,
As birds welcome back the longer days,
So this light keeps breaking in.
Piercing the darkness, lightening the gloom,
Searching out and shining into the pain.

Could it be, at last, after waiting so long,
I am beginning to see again, to breathe again, to live again?
Could it be that?

I wrote those words 26 months after Jim had died; and now, two years later, although there are always ups and downs, I still feel that time marked the point where I began to live again. It is amazing for me to reflect on that now, and to see how I was kept safe through such a long period of desolation and desperation. I offer the words now in the hope that someone else may connect and know that they are not forgotten in their darkness and dare to believe that light will one day pierce the gloom.

Waiting

It is never easy to be told to wait. We tend to want things when we want them, and this has become known as an age where we look for instant gratification. This is understandable . . . who wants to wait for what they know they want and need? Recently, Graeme and I had a lovely experience that made us chuckle. We were in a café linked to a small museum in London and watched as a mum came in with a baby in a buggy and a delightful little bespectacled boy of about three. She sat him down and told him to wait and not to touch anything while she went to the nearby counter to order some drinks. Suddenly the little chap noticed the bowl of sugar lumps in front of him. We could see the cogs of his brain actually turning at that point! He knew very well he wasn't meant to touch them, but he so wanted to. In the end, after wrestling with his conscience for a while, he slowly reached out a hand, surreptitiously collected a sugar lump, gave it a delicate lick and then replaced it very gently in the bowl. This process was repeated several times but he never actually ate one, so he thought he had done quite well! When his mum returned we wondered whether we should split on him, but really he just looked too cute in his glasses.

Unwelcome though we usually find it, waiting can have an important place in our life journeys, or indeed in our life gardens. Sometimes, in barren times there is nothing we can do except wait and trust that, though it is terribly hard, God has not forgotten us, and one day it will feel easier. The Bible is full of men and women waiting and wondering why God has not heard and answered their prayers sooner. I am reminded of Mary and Martha at the tomb of their brother, Lazarus.[1] They waited two or three days for Jesus to arrive even though they had called for him earlier, and when he did arrive they asked him why he had taken so long. They were unable to understand why they had to wait. Returning to the metaphor of the garden or a field, we often sow seed on to damp, dark soil, and have to wait a long time before there is any harvest. Even then there are the dangers of slugs or bugs or too much rain or sun which might choke our best attempts. There are so many situations in which we wait in apparent darkness, and it is always hard. There is positive waiting such as in pregnancy, when hopefully there will be happy results; and then there is the more negative waiting, where we are flung into what feels like a dark hole and we wonder if we will ever get out. It may be that in those dark, secret, places God is at work in us to transform us, and when we eventually make it back to the light, things will look different. One bereaved father wrote of waiting thus:

I hardly knew what I was waiting for. I called upon God the comforter, but God did not come. I cried out to the void, and heard only the silence. Still, I went on with my life – my work, my family, my worship, my politics. And . . . I began to hear some new sounds – my own laughter, my own singing, my own sounds of joy. I listened to myself, and heard the power of God's 'Yes' prevailing amidst my sorrow and pain, and I knew that God the comforter had never left me.[2]

We also need to be prepared to wait with our bereaved friends, or those in any kind of deep emotional distress, and it isn't easy. It is hard to see people we care about suffer, and we naturally want to do something or say something to try and make things better, but often we can help most by just being with them and accompanying them on their long, slow progress to recovery for as long as it takes. Nicholas Wolterstorff, in *Lament for a Son*, likens this to just sitting beside them, on what he calls the 'mourning bench', rather than 'doing' anything.[3]

I think those of us who profess to be Christians need to be particularly careful how we use our well-intentioned words. It is not helpful to be told that God must have felt that Jim, or whoever, had done all he was meant to do on earth and now he has been taken to a better place. When a child or an adult dies young, everything in you screams, 'No, this is wrong; it can't be – there was so much more he could have done'. Nor is it helpful to be reminded that you will see your loved one again one day . . . all that matters to you in times of great pain is that you can't see him or talk to him now and that you won't see him grow up, get a job, maybe marry and have children of his own. The future is just too far away to contemplate at such a time. I can understand and sympathise with why we try to pour oil on troubled waters in these ways, and I fear I have done the same thing myself more times than I care to remember; but we need to think carefully about the impact of our words. Sometimes it may be better to say nothing and to be a companion in silence or else to simply listen and to try to resist the temptation to find an explanation.

For me personally, I had to put up with waiting, times of darkness and seeming inactivity, not knowing exactly what I was waiting for nor what may come of it. Not only was I trying to survive in the aftermath of losing Jim, but in other areas of my life I was also experiencing deep frustration and disappointment. Seventeen months after Jim died and just two weeks after my father died, I wrote:

It's Easter time here – all seems unreal and suspended just now. Everything hanging, everything waiting.

I am waiting, waiting, waiting for something, but I don't know what . . . I just wait for the glimmer of a way forward . . . Wouldn't it be wonderful to have something good to write, something worth writing about, something to give joy? One day that will surely be the case. I wait in hope.

Nearly three years later I can look back and see how that time of waiting was not wasted. So much has changed since then in me and for me. I know, however, that any work of transformation is still very much a work in progress and it's going to be a slow, hard job. Like the heavy clay soil in my garden which does not absorb the water well, and makes it hard for many things to grow, I can be a bit dense to say the least and things take a long time to sink in. I think I need a fair bit of compost mixed in to lighten me up and nourish me – not a very comfortable process!

Continuing bonds

I thank God for the day when, after much searching on the internet for something to help me in understanding how to live with bereavement, I discovered the concept of continuing bonds, a term which has been written about, with reference to bereaved parents, by Dennis Klaas.[4] This model of grief, first described in the early 1990s, built on the work of earlier grief researchers, merely made acceptable in academic and grief professional circles what bereaved people already knew from experience. Our relationship with the person we loved while they were alive carries on in a changed form after death. Previously, through the work of Freud and others, who were usually relating to patients with serious mental health issues, it had been assumed that the way to recover from grief healthily was to sever emotional bonds with the deceased and to put your energies into building new relationships. That sounds so cruel, and now it was recognised that in reality this is not what happens. Each bereaved person, lamenting the loss of someone very important to them, will in time find their own way of maintaining that relationship. The person you loved in life is still part of who you are. You are partly who you are because of that relationship, and now that she or he is gone, that doesn't change. You still have a relationship, you still love them, they still have an impact on the way you live.

I find this very liberating – now I understand that I don't have to 'get over it' but that I can work out my own way of continuing a relationship that was and is important to me. So, as mentioned earlier, I often have a bunch of lilies in the hall and I have objects and pictures around that are meaningful to me and are special in relationship to Jim. They connect me to him, as does writing his story and my response to it. No longer do bereaved people have to meekly accept the opinions of experts who tell them they should do this or should be like that, or else they risk being labelled – terrible term – 'stuck in their bereavement'.[5] I love the story found in the book, *New Journeys Now Begin* (a really warm and humane book), which clearly shows how the feelings and wisdom of bereaved people can be disregarded by those who think they know better:

I worked with one widow in her later years who was labelled by her doctor as exhibiting signs of denying the loss of her husband and being unwilling to move on from it because she still kept his toothbrush beside hers in the bathroom. She told me she kept the toothbrush there not only because it had always been there, but also because, first thing in the morning it reminded her of her husband. Of course she knew her husband was dead. She wasn't hanging on to him in any way or denying he was gone. She was simply holding on to those things, a toothbrush included, which reminded her of what it had been like when her husband was around.[6]

Each person will find their own way. There are no rights or wrongs in this and it is hardly a new idea, just recognition by experts that this is what happens. Most people will become their own experts in how to keep a meaningful connection with their loved one. In old days it was common to wear a locket, perhaps with a lock of hair or a miniature portrait; now we will find any number of creative ways of doing what is important to us – from planting trees, to writing books, to running a marathon, to starting a charity in their honour.

As a Christian, I have to accept that my own faith tradition has not always been very helpful in recognising our human need of a continuing bond in the here and now. Perhaps this is because Western expressions of Christianity have been so heavily influenced by ancient Greek thought, with its tendency to separate the spiritual from the material and to elevate the former over the latter. Such a dualistic way of thinking can lead to a whitewashing of our losses. 'Well, he is safe now in the arms of Jesus and you will see him again one day.' This may well be true, but the fact remains that we are thoroughly physical beings as well as spiritual and we feel our losses physically as well. I think it is perfectly possible to live with a foot in both camps. I can learn to leave Jim with Jesus spiritually (though it hasn't been easy) and at the same time I am free to recognise my terrible human loss and find ways of carrying Jim with me in the present world, that help me live more easily.

Dancing with hope

Nearly a year after Jim died, Graeme and I had a very peaceful and much-needed holiday in Cornwall. We were both exhausted after a very heavy year and it was wonderful at last to be able to walk away from all the demands of daily life. We had many long clifftop walks, enjoying the beauty and spectacle of the wild coastline. We found that we just talked and talked about the events of the previous eleven months, as we tried to integrate what had happened into our lives and still struggled with understanding how it could all have gone so wrong.

As we descended into one little cove, we noticed a rather abandoned looking, nondescript hut. Being inveterately curious, I couldn't resist peering through the window, just in case there was something interesting inside. There wasn't much, old fishing nets, lobster pots and broken chairs and the like, but on the outside there was a piece of A4 paper with the following words typed on it:

Hope is the ability to hear the music of the future and faith is having the courage to dance to it now.

Peter Kusmic.[7]

Those words smacked me between the eyes. I knew they were important for me and I learnt them by heart straight away, and when I got home I wrote them in my journal. In those words was another clue to surviving in my new world. God was inviting me to dance with him in the here and now, not content with me putting my life on hold until one day we would meet again and have all the answers.

But what did that mean, in reality? It wasn't an immediate solution to my struggle with grief but I knew it was something I had to mull over and give thought to. A few weeks after Jim died I had written to him:

Now I have to dance without you and it hurts me. Now we have to carry on the dance, but it doesn't feel right, clumsy and out of balance. You were part of my dance Jim and without you I am wrong footed . . . Somehow I have to learn to dance again . . . What kind of dance do I want? Dull, slow, clumsy, leaden footed – or sure, bright, confident, carrying you into the future, as well as myself?

111

Now God was saying to me, very clearly, literally in black and white, you can dance right now, if you keep hold of hope. Though I was still actively grieving, the future began to feel like somewhere I could one day live.

Living creatively

Yet another book was brought to my attention not long after this. Tom Wright's *Surprised by Hope*, though not what you would call a quick read for a bereaved person, showed me a way of thinking about the world and the world to come that really gave me something to build on.[8] The book argues, controversially for some, that the Kingdom of God will be right here, not in some far-off heaven, but rebuilt out of the stuff we all know and love – earth, water, man, woman, animals, trees and so on, but without death, tears, mourning and other forms of pain and suffering. I am not a theologian, and the scope of this particular book is very wide and not written with bereavement in mind, so for me to refer to it in my much narrower context makes me feel a little nervous. Nevertheless, for me it lived up to its title in that it helped me understand how I could play my own small role in contributing to building the Kingdom of God here on earth, and in so doing I was looking forward to that time when there would be a new heaven and a new earth, with no more tears, when one day I would understand and would be reunited with my Jim, right here, in a flesh and blood sense. Tom Wright helped me to understand that every creative act, however small, was part of building that Kingdom. When I was living in days where sometimes the most creative and challenging thing I would do was to step into the garden and feed the birds, that was a message I needed to hear. In undertaking such small actions, I was declaring that I was not redundant, and I still had a role to play.

I believe that God speaks to us in many different ways, and

it seems I 'hear' most clearly when I am out and about, rather than enmeshed in daily concerns. On one occasion, nearly two years after Jim died, I was away on a conference. I slipped out for an early-morning breather and was walking through a rural churchyard, talking to Graeme on my mobile. Big on our minds at that moment was the question of what next – where do we go from here? I glanced up at the church as I followed the path round the crooked gravestones. There I noticed a beautiful modern clock, given in commemoration of the millennium, and written above it in bold lettering were the words, 'Do not forget to live'. I felt that God was saying to me, 'Come on, this has happened, but you still have a life. Get out there and live it as well as you can'.

Some four years and more after Jim died, my life is moving forward and I am now involved in a number of new initiatives which have helped me to slowly get back on my feet and through which I can contribute in small ways. I have not forgotten the messages of the fishermen's hut, the book and the clock, and I celebrate each creative act, however small, for what it heralds in the bigger context.

Weaving acceptance

In our bedroom we have a beautiful wallhanging, hand woven in silk by a tribeswoman in the north of Thailand, using traditional methods and natural dyes. As such, it is unique. We bought it while on a visit to Graeme's father who lived in Thailand and it reminds me that life is full of uncertainties, as when an item is made in such a way some irregularities in pattern and colour are inevitable. As I have told our story in these pages, it has struck me how the words and the order in which I have chosen to write them also represent a weaving, as one idea has led to another, and sometimes I have looped back and then jumped forward. There is a pattern and an order, but it is not predictable and the result is something that is also unique, as everybody's story is.

Nearly three years after Jim died, I discovered that the metaphor of weaving was helpful in the context of thinking about bereavement in another way too. I learnt that the word 'accept' has its roots in an Anglo-Saxon term related to the weaving process.[9] Bereaved people often feel uncomfortable about the idea of acceptance. What does it mean to 'accept' the death of a loved one? I felt I could never accept Jim's death, which was an event that was so clearly wrong. Now I discovered another way of thinking about acceptance that made more sense to me. Apparently when a weaver made a mistake it wasn't always possible to put it right without risking destroying the whole fabric. Instead she had to find a way of working with what she had; she had to accept or grasp the thread that was wrong and work it into the fabric so that what she ended up with was not what she had planned, but was still good and useable. For me, this spoke of my recognition that though I wouldn't and couldn't meekly accept Jim's death, I could choose to live positively with the unalterable fact, and weave his loss into the fabric of my life.

So that is what I am working on now, fully aware that this piece of fabric, the story of one ordinary life, remains unfinished and is still being woven. When I started out weaving all those years ago, I did not know the complexity of the colours, textures and patterns that this simple piece of material would hold. The most unpromising and ordinary material can, transformed by the grace of God, become something deeper, richer and more valuable than we could imagine. For now, I keep on going, learning new things all the time, travelling on in my life without Jim, but resolutely carrying him in my heart, which I am proud to do.

I have learnt that though, as far as I am concerned, his death was a meaningless waste and the result of the spiritual battle we are all in in this world, his young life wasn't wasted, and even in his dying there may be new life for others that I may never know about. This does not make his loss easier to bear, but it remains a fact. I have discovered many things along the way of grief that have deepened my appreciation of the world around me and, hopefully, my compassion for others. I have had many of my assumptions shaken to the core, and I have had to come face to face with the world of drugs, let it affect me and not keep the seamier sides of life at arm's length, something that is so easy to do when you live a comfortable sort of life. I know I face a daily challenge to keep involved and not to turn away from injustice and marginalisation wherever I know that it exists – whether through drugs or other issues. Jim helped to teach me this, through his way of life and his way of death.

As I worked my way through this chapter, and then checked and reviewed what I had written, I was struck by the fact that, unplanned, all the subtitles were written using the present participle (once an English teacher, always an English teacher!) – waiting, continuing, dancing, living, weaving. How appropriate this seems to me . . . my life is active and continuing in a variety of positive ways. I believe, by the grace of God, I have been able to weave in losing Jim as part of my life, and though it is the opposite of what I would have chosen, his death has made me stronger. The truth remains that I would choose to have him back today if I could, but I can't, so I needs must make what I can of the life I have until I see him again and understand more fully. So perhaps, finally, I am finding some cosmos, some harmony, some sense of flourishing despite the pain and sorrow, and I thank God for this.

I am profoundly grateful for my beloved Graeme, our children and now our three children-in-law who have walked with us on this sorry journey and who continue to inspire us with their determination to keep going and to make a difference to their own parts of the world. I know I am blessed, it is undeserved and I am thankful.

I'll finish with a few words I wrote to Jim, just about that time when I began to feel I could live again, and trust that for someone else the words may carry some hope and meaning as they begin to step out on their own journey to living again after loss:

Bonded together but not tied,
Separated in time and space but as close in spirit
As a mother carrying her unborn child.
Two, but inseparable –
You freer than you've ever been,
Me, letting go but holding on to love,
'Love never ends . . .
And now faith, hope and love abide, these three,
And the greatest of these is love.'

God bless you, hold you and be with you, Jim, until we meet again. Love, always. Mum xx

POSTSCRIPT 1

Meeting Bill

As part of our own recovery process and hopefully as a way of helping and connecting with others who had had or were having hard times in their own lives, Graeme and I put together a few presentations and seminars, two to three years after Jim died, on the issue of bereavement and more particularly the issue of bereavement by drugs. At one of these, given at the New Wine summer conference in Newark in 2010, we had an extraordinary meeting. I was so amazed by this that as soon as I got access to a computer I wrote it down and shared it, with permission from Bill, with a number of friends. I include it here, in the same form that I wrote in then, written in the heat and excitement of the moment.

After Jim died in November 2007, Graeme and I spent considerable time looking up all the contacts he had recently had in his last months in Hong Kong. We were desperate for information, anything that would give us extra clues into how he was and what was going on in his life. We managed to make contact with many people, and occasionally we found ourselves contacted out of the blue by someone we didn't know, but who knew Jim, and wanted to share time and stories with us. All of these links were very comforting to us, and over the months we were able to put together stories like the pieces of a jigsaw, until we had quite a full picture of how he had seemed to others and what was going on for him. Ironically, between such stories, our own letters and emails received from him and his diaries, we found ourselves in the strange situation as parents of knowing probably more than you usually would about your 21-year-old son! What was most encouraging for us was how the stories, told by many different people of all ages and nationalities, had a consistent thread. They spoke about the Jim we knew and loved, the Jim who was a loving, puzzling enigma, who knew himself to be deeply loved by God and others and yet who had deep sadness mixed in with his cheeky, droll personality.

However, there was one contact that eluded us. We had a letter written by a man called Bill found among Jim's possessions which said quite a lot and was warm and encouraging. He had clearly had a good bond with Jim and we were keen to know who he was, to glean information and to say 'Thank you' for caring about him. Nobody seemed to know who Bill was, so we were stuck. We just kept the letter along with other mementoes in the chest of drawers in our bedroom which we had put aside for the purpose. There it sat for nearly three years, an unsolved mystery.

This year Graeme and I were invited to speak at a seminar at New Wine about addiction, loss and finding hope. Naturally, it was quite a nerve-wracking thing to do as we tackled difficult personal and emotional territory with a large group of people we didn't know and who didn't know us. It seemed to be going quite well, when a man walked in a bit late, came almost to the front of the large room and sat down. Fifteen minutes from the end, he raised a hand. I am not a seasoned speaker so was some-what floored by this. I asked what he wanted and he asked if he could give a testimony. I am nothing if not a well-organised person, and as far as I was concerned I wanted to say what I had planned, so I suggested he waited till the end and was relieved when he agreed to this.

Well, there wasn't time in the end, and after we had finished our bit, Graeme made a bee-line for the man. Then we felt quite relieved we had not agreed for him to talk in the meeting – we would have been overwhelmed. This was Bill, whose letter was still sitting in our bedroom drawer. He wanted to tell how he had known Jim and how the relationship had been deeply significant. He numbered Jim among four or five most influential friends in his life, and following his time with him in Hong Kong, had changed direction in his life, done a counselling course and was now working with young men with drug addiction problems. That was all amazing enough, but then we realised how extraordinary it was that he had been in a position to attend the meeting.

Bill had come up from the south of England to New Wine North for the week, to work on a charity stall in the market place. He had nipped out to use the loo and while he was passing the room where we were speaking he noticed the topic was on drugs – an area of interest for him. Then to his surprise he heard Hong Kong mentioned and his ears pricked up even more as he had visited there and worked with recovering addicts. Then, to his astonishment he heard Jim's name – and at that point dissolved in tears. He phoned his wife to excuse himself from the stall for a while as he knew he had to stay and listen. Hence he walked in late and positioned himself near the front of the room.

Bill had only discovered that Jim had died six months after the event, and had been very distressed. He felt a burden of guilt, as so many of us did, that he hadn't been able to support him more. He had photos and a letter from Jim kept in a Bible that he has never been able to open since, as it was too upsetting for him. Now here he was, with Jim's parents, able to talk about these things, share the pain and make a bit more sense of what had happened. For him it was clearly a very moving and healing encounter. How wonderful was that?

What did it mean for us, the parents, who are determined to speak out about drugs and loss and keeping hope in Jesus? It just seemed like an enormous gift. Nearly three years later, as we are beginning this new part of our lives, it felt very much that God was saying, 'I'm still with you in all of this . . . walking with you day by day'. It was a totally unlooked for and unexpected blessing, and the answer to an unsolved part of the puzzle. Wonderful! And it is so heartening to hear yet more of how much Jim was loved, how he had an influence on many individuals and how that influence goes on. He does not seem dead to us, with stories like this. Finally, how encouraging to hear again about how Jim had spoken of all his family with love and pleasure. How reassuring for us – what a great God we have who communicates with us in so many different ways, and always finds ways to remind us he is with us.

Praise to God!

David's Letter

There is one person missing from this story – David, the man that Jim was with when he died. For a long time I didn't know how to think about him. I knew what he looked like well enough, because there he was in so many photos next to Jim, as they larked about together. I also knew a little about him, as Jim had often referred to him in his later emails. As far as Jim was concerned he was a real friend, and Jim cared about him.

When we heard that Jim had chosen to go to David's flat and that he had died there, it was hard to imagine what had happened and in many ways better not to. Since we didn't know and never could, it was perhaps kinder not to let our minds play on imagined scenarios, if we could help it.

We were aware that David attended Jim's memorial service a week after he died, slipping in late and leaving early, carefully avoiding any contact with us. After that, we had nothing except a vacuum. The question hung in our minds – should we be angry with this person? Could he have done anything to prevent the death? How could we forgive him . . . Or was there any need to forgive him anyway? Perhaps we should just feel sad for him? I looked at the photos and wondered if I should cut him out of them, but then remembered that Jim had cared for him, they had been good friends, and to cut up the photos would probably upset Jim if he knew about it.

When we returned to Hong Kong sixteen months after Jim

died, we wondered whether we should try to make contact with him, but we were told that David had moved on in his life, got married and started a business, and we felt that it would be a difficult meeting for all involved. So, finally, we left it. We put the questions out of our mind, kept the photos as they were and just tried to get on with our lives, needing to be content with the 'not knowing'. Still, in my heart I kept wondering what had happened, and, most painful of all to me, wondering if David had actually cared about Jim or whether Jim in his occasional naïvety in his choice of friends had just got it wrong. The thought that Jim might have died in the presence of someone who didn't care about him was one of the most painful feelings for me. I wanted to forgive, but in the absence of any information it was hard to do so, as I didn't know what I was needing to forgive.

Three years later to the day of Jim's memorial service a letter arrived. We didn't even look at it until dusk as we were both busy with our own lives. When we finally sat down and looked at the day's post, we swallowed a bit when we realised from the address that one letter had come from the community rehabilitation house in Hong Kong and was in fact from David. We opened it with some anxiety, simply not knowing what to expect. Now, in the most courteous of ways, David expressed his sorrow for our loss and regret for the fact that he had felt unable to contact us earlier or to speak with us face to face. As he said, it was just too difficult for him. Now, three years later, he wrote about his affection for Jim and how he felt the tragedy of his young death. He described the events of that fateful night and ended by once again expressing his sorrow and inviting us to contact him if we wanted to know any more.

At last, we had a better picture of what had happened. Having the facts, at least as David saw them, made no practical difference of course, except in one very important area. It was clear that David had felt great affection for Jim, had wanted to save him and do his best for him, and that he had valued his younger friend. It is clear too that Jim, on that night when he felt lost and alone, made a wrong choice as David was caught in the mire of drugs and also made wrong decisions.

We recognised just how much courage it must have taken him to write. After so long it would have been easier just to leave things as they were. He must have realised by then that we never expected to hear from him so there was no obligation on him. After we had got over the shock of receiving the letter, we were grateful that another area of unknowing and uncertainty had been cleared up for us, and I was grateful that I now felt freer to feel for Jim's friend and to look at his photo.

I wrote to David, by return of post, to thank him for writing and to acknowledge his courage in doing so – especially as English wasn't his first language, which made the task harder than it would have been. I feel sad for him that his life has not gone smoothly since that time either, as he has returned to the rehabilitation house. I know how that would upset Jim who had longed to be able to support him in recovery.

So David, if you should ever read this, thank you again for writing, God be with you and may you yet find the strength to walk free from the curse of drugs, free to be the man you are made to be.

Notes

Chapter 1
1. To discover more about New Wine and how it has developed, go to www. new-wine.org.

Chapter 2
1. http://rds.homeoffice.gov.uk/rds/pdfs09/hosb1209.pdf, accessed 17 February 2011.
2. To find out about Jackie Pullinger and the work she has done for many years in Hong Kong and elsewhere, read her book *Chasing the Dragon*.
3. For helpful background information on drugs, go to www.talktofrank. com.

Chapter 3
1. www.rcpsych.ac.uk/mentalhealthinfo/problems/alcoholandrugs/ cannabis.aspx, accessed 22 February 2011.

Chapter 4
1. Reproduced by kind permission of Kingsway publishers.

Chapter 5
1. Eugene Peterson, *A Long Obedience in the Same Direction* (Downers Grove, IL 60515, IVP 2000), p. 119.

Chapter 6
1. Irvin D. Yalom, *Love's Executioner* (London, Penguin Books, 1991), p. 139.
2. Dennis Klaas, *The Spiritual Lives of Bereaved Parents* (Philadelphia PA19106, Taylor and Francis, 1999), p. 11.
3. Dietrich Bonhoeffer quoted in Dave Tomlinson, *Running into God* (London, SPCK, 2004), p. 102.
4. Ronald Dunn, *When Heaven is Silent* (Milton Keynes, Nelson Word, 1994), p. 21.
5. Richard Rohr, *Everything Belongs* (New York NY10001, Crossroad Publishing Company, 2003), p. 46.

6. www.hospiceslo.org/lib_resourcecenter/articles/wordenstasks.html, accessed 17 February 2011.
7. Harold S. Kushner, *When Bad things Happen to Good People* (New York, Anchor Books, 2004)
8. Nicholas Wolterstorff, *Lament for a Son* (Grand Rapids, Michigan, Wm B. Eerdmans Publishing Co., 1987).
9. Habakkuk 3.17–19.
10. Eugene Peterson, *A Long Obedience in the Same Direction* (Downers Grove, IL60515, IVP, 2000 edition), p. 134.
11. To learn more about Care for the Family go to www.careforthefamily.org.uk.
12. Found in Mary Oliver, *Thirst* (Highgreen, Tarset, Northumberland, BloodAxe Books, 2007).

Chapter 7
1. *The Guardian*, 5 April 2008.
2. www.thesun.co.uk/sol/homepage/showbiz/tv/2005666/Last-video-diary-of-a-heroin-addict-from-a-loving-home.html, accessed 23 February 2011.
3. Elizabeth Burton-Phillips, *Mum, Can You Lend Me Twenty Quid?* (London, Piatkus, 2007).
4. To learn more about DrugFam go to www.drugfam.co.uk.
5. Dave Bookless, *God Doesn't Do Waste* (Nottingham, IVP, 2010), p. 70.

Chapter 8
1. Steve Griffiths, *God of the Valley* (Oxford, The Bible Reading Fellowship, 2003), p. 68.
2. Victor Frankl, *Man's Search for Meaning* (UK, Ebury Press, 2004 edition). A classic book on finding meaning for life in the midst of suffering, based on the writer's experiences as a prisoner in a concentration camp during the Second World War.
3. Henri J. M. Nouwen, *The Wounded Healer* (London, Darton, Longman and Todd, 2007 edition). Another classic text.
4. Tom Gordon, *New Journeys Now Begin* (Glasgow, Wild Goose Publications, 2006), p. 140.
5. Pete Greig, *God on Mute* (Eastbourne, Survivor, 2007), p. 103.
6. Walter Brueggemann, *The Psalms and the Life of Faith* (Minneapolis, Fortress Press, 1995).
7. John Pritchard, *God Lost and Found* (London, SPCK, 2011), p. 57.
8. Steve Griffiths, *God of the Valley* (Oxford, The Bible Reading Fellowship, 2003), p. 80.
9. For more information on DR Congo and Pat Nickson see www.diamonds-in-the-darkness.co.uk. For a wider view see Richard Dowden, *Africa, Altered States, Ordinary Miracles* (Holland Park, London, Portobello Books, 2008).

Chapter 9

1. John 11.
2. Mary Cobb and friends, *Waiting and Being* (Louisville, KY40207, Fons Vitae, 2010), p. 47.
3. Nicholas Wolterstorff, *Lament for a Son* (Grand Rapids, Michigan, Wm B. Eerdmans Publishing Co., 1987), p. 34.
4. Dennis Klaas, *The Spiritual Lives of Bereaved Parents* (Philadelphia PA19106, Taylor and Francis, 1999).
5. Some people will require extra expert help to support them in their loss, of course.
6. Tom Gordon, *New Journeys Now Begin* (Glasgow, Wild Goose Publications, 2006), p. 159.
7. I am not sure where this quote is found but I have since discovered that Peter Kusmic, the author, is a well-respected theologian from Croatia.
8. Tom Wright, *Surprised by Hope* (London, SPCK, 2007).
9. I thank Libby Purves, the journalist, for this wonderful metaphor found at: www.dailymail.co.uk/home/you/article-1169947/Libby-Purves-8216-There-solution-grief-8217.html, accessed 13 April 2011.